KILLARNEY TRAVEL GU

DISCOVER AND EXPLORE THE GATEWAY TO THE RING OF KERRY

REX M. JASON

Copyright © 2025 by Rex M. Jason

All rights reserved. No part of this book may be reproduced, stored in a retrieval system, or transmitted in any form or by any means, electronic, mechanical, photocopying, recording, or otherwise, without the prior written permission of the publisher.

WOULD YOU LIKE TO GET INSTANT ACCESS TO MORE TRAVEL GUIDE BOOKS BY THE AUTHOR? SCAN THE QR CODE BELOW!

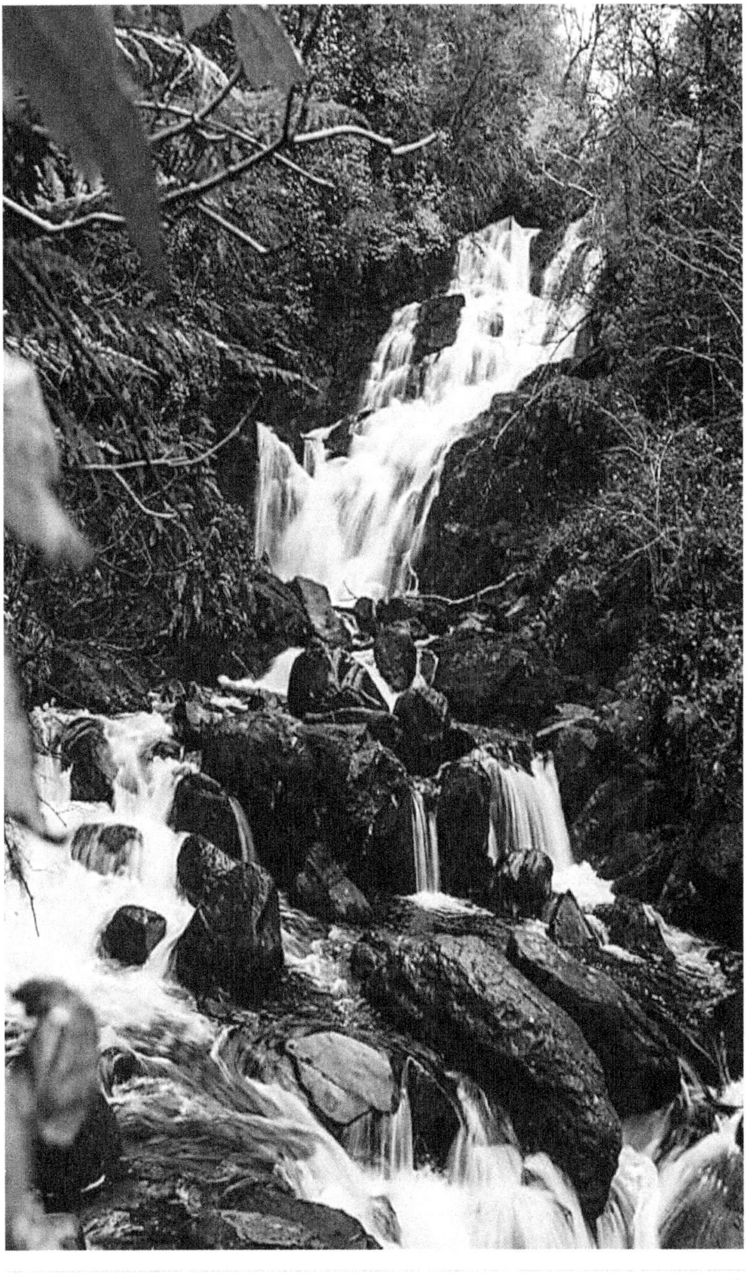

TABLE OF CONTENTS

INTRODUCTION 7

CHAPTER 1 10

    OVERVIEW OF KILLARNEY 10

    WHY VISIT KILLARNEY? 10

    FUN FACTS ABOUT KILLARNEY 12

    GEOGRAPHY AND CLIMATE 15

CHAPTER 2 17

    PLANNING YOUR TRIP 17

    GETTING TO KILLARNEY 18

    VISA REQUIREMENTS 20

    ACCOMMODATIONS FOR ANY BUDGET AND STYLE 23

    WHEN TO VISIT 27

    ESSENTIAL PACKAGING LIST 31

CHAPTER 3 34

    GETTING AROUND KILLARNEY 34

    PUBLIC TRANSPORTATION 35

RENTING A CAR 37
CYCLING 41
WALKING TOURS 44

CHAPTER 4 48

EATING AND DRINKING IN KILLARNEY 48
TRADITIONAL IRISH CUISINE 49
RESTAURANTS 52
LOCAL SPECIALTIES 56

CHAPTER 5 60

TOP ATTRACTIONS IN KILLARNEY 60
KILLARNEY NATIONAL PARK 61
MUCKROSS HOUSE AND GARDENS 64
TORC WATERFALL 68
ROSS CASTLE 72
GAP IN DUNLOE 75
RING OF KERRY 78
THE SKELLIG ISLANDS 82
KILLARNEY LAKES 86
JAUNTING CARS 89

CHAPTER 6 93

ACTIVITIES IN KILLARNEY 93
HIKING AND WALKING TRAILS 94
CYCLING ROUTES 97
GOLFING 101
WATER ACTIVITIES 104
HORSE RIDING 106
TRADITIONAL IRISH MUSIC AND DANCE 110

CHAPTER 7 113

SHOPPING IN KILLARNEY 113
SOUVENIRS 114
LOCAL CRAFTS 117
MARKETS 121

CHAPTER 8 124

PRACTICAL INFORMATION 124
STAYING CONNECTED: INTERNET AND MOBILE
COMMUNICATION 125
LAWS AND REGULATIONS 128
CURRENCY AND MONEY-SAVING TIPS 131

SAFETY AND SECURITY 134
HEALTH AND MEDICAL ASSISTANCE 137
SUSTAINABLE TOURISM 140
USEFUL PHRASES IN IRISH GAELIC 144

CONCLUSION 147

INTRODUCTION

Killarney, located in the rugged southwestern region of Ireland, is a timeless oasis where ancient legends mingle with whispers of a captivating past. This enchanting town, nestled between the majestic MacGillycuddy's Reeks and the shimmering lakes of Killarney National Park, has long served as a beacon for those seeking to discover Ireland's rich history.

The history of Killarney begins in the mists of antiquity when the ancient Celts left their mark on the land. The legendary warrior-queen Maeve once ruled here, among the rolling hills and shimmering waters, her fierce spirit casting a spell over the rugged terrain. Her exploits, immortalized in the great Irish epic Táin Bó Cúailnge, have captivated generations of imaginations, and the echoes of her legacy still linger in the air.

Killarney's strategic location on ancient trade routes attracted the attention of powerful dynasties over the centuries. The Norman invaders, led by the renowned knight Sir Eoghan O'Sullivan, established a stronghold in the region, with towering castles and fortified manors demonstrating their ambition. During this turbulent period, the iconic Ross Castle, with its striking silhouette against the shimmering waters of Lough Leane, began to take shape, its walls bearing witness to the ebb and flow of conflict that defined Ireland's history. However, Killarney's story is more than just one of conquest and turmoil. It is also a story about resilience, cultural diversity, and the enduring spirit of its people. The region's natural beauty, with its lush forests, cascading waterfalls, and tranquil lakes, has long captivated the hearts of artists, poets, and tourists. Killarney was the birthplace of Ireland's Romantic movement, with luminaries such as William Wordsworth and Sir Walter Scott paying tribute to the town's enchanting landscapes.

Killarney is a living testament to the enduring strength of Ireland's cultural heritage. As you wander its cobbled streets, discover the hidden gems of its thriving arts scene, and bask in the warmth of its hospitality, you will be drawn into a tapestry of legends and history with the power to inspire and captivate. This travel guide will help you unlock the secrets of this extraordinary place, inviting you on a journey of discovery that will leave an indelible mark on your heart and soul.

CHAPTER 1

OVERVIEW OF KILLARNEY

WHY VISIT KILLARNEY?

As a traveler looking to immerse yourself in Ireland's rich tapestry of cultural heritage and breathtaking natural landscapes, there is no better place than the enchanting town of Killarney. The first and most compelling reason for visiting Killarney is its breathtaking natural beauty. This town, nestled between the majestic MacGillycuddy's Reeks and the shimmering lakes of Killarney National Park, is a veritable oasis of tranquility and wonder.

The park, a UNESCO World Heritage site, is a vast expanse of pristine wilderness ripe for exploration. Killarney's natural landscapes are truly breathtaking, from ancient forests and cascading waterfalls to serene, mirror-like lakes. But Killarney's appeal goes far beyond its natural wonders. The town is also a living testament to Ireland's rich cultural heritage, with a thriving arts scene that honors the country's musical, dancing, and storytelling traditions. The Killarney Folk Festival, held every summer, is a prime example of this cultural vibrancy, attracting visitors from all over the world to experience the energy and warmth of the town's vibrant community.

As you walk through Killarney's charming streets, you'll be transported back in time, immersed in the town's rich history and the echoes of ancient legends that still reverberate. Killarney is rich in history, from the iconic Ross Castle to the legendary warrior-queen Maeve, whose exploits were immortalized in the great Irish epic, the Táin Bó Cúailnge. Beyond the town itself, the surrounding region provides numerous opportunities for adventure and exploration. Perhaps most importantly, Killarney embodies the warmth and hospitality that Ireland is known for.

The town's vibrant community of residents takes great pride in sharing their traditions and stories with visitors, resulting in an atmosphere of genuine welcome and camaraderie that is simply unparalleled. Whether you're looking for a peaceful escape from the stresses of everyday life, a deep dive into Ireland's captivating history and culture, or an adventure-filled exploration of the great outdoors, Killarney provides a truly unique and unforgettable experience.

FUN FACTS ABOUT KILLARNEY

As a traveler embarking on a journey through the captivating town of Killarney, Ireland, you'll quickly realize that there's much more to this enchanting destination than meets the eye. Beneath the surface of its breathtaking natural beauty and rich cultural heritage, there is a treasure trove of fascinating facts that will captivate you and leave you wanting to learn more.

Killarney is notable for being the birthplace of Ireland's Romantic movement. In the early nineteenth century, the town's breathtaking landscapes and picturesque charm captivated the imaginations of renowned poets and writers such as William Wordsworth and Sir Walter Scott.

Their inspired works contributed to Killarney's reputation as a muse for artists and a destination that celebrated nature's ability to move the human spirit. Speaking of nature, the town's crown jewel is unquestionably Killarney National Park, a vast expanse of pristine wilderness that has been designated a UNESCO World Heritage site. Its ancient forests and shimmering lakes are home to a diverse range of wildlife, including the iconic red deer, Ireland's only wild deer herd. These majestic creatures have roamed the region for centuries, demonstrating the timeless beauty of Killarney's natural landscapes.

Another fascinating fact about Killarney is its long history as a strategic location on ancient trade routes. Over the centuries, the town has seen numerous battles and conflicts as powerful dynasties competed for control of the region. This turbulent past is most visible in the iconic Ross Castle, which serves as a silent witness to the town's illustrious history. Built by the powerful O'Donoghue clan in the 15th century, the castle's walls have witnessed the ebb and flow of conflict, from Norman invasions to Irish rebellions that shaped Ireland's history. However, Killarney's history is not entirely about conflict and conquest.

The town has also served as a cultural and artistic hub, with a thriving arts scene that honors Irish music, dance, and storytelling traditions. One of the town's most popular annual events is the Killarney Folk Festival, a vibrant celebration of the country's rich folk heritage that attracts visitors from all over the world.

Perhaps one of the most delightful aspects of Killarney is its people's unwavering warmth and hospitality. The town's residents take great pride in sharing their traditions and stories with visitors, resulting in an atmosphere of genuine welcome and camaraderie that is simply unparalleled.

Whether you're drinking a pint in a cozy pub, strolling through Killarney's charming streets, or engaging in lively conversation with a local, you'll quickly realize that the true heart of Killarney is found in the warmth and generosity of its residents. As you immerse yourself in Killarney's captivating world, these and other fascinating facts will emerge, providing a deeper understanding and appreciation for this extraordinary Irish gem.

GEOGRAPHY AND CLIMATE

Killarney's geographical significance is centered on the stunning Killarney National Park, a vast expanse of pristine wilderness designated as a UNESCO World Heritage site. The park, which spans an impressive 26,000 hectares, exemplifies the power and beauty of Ireland's natural heritage, displaying a diverse range of landscapes that have captivated visitors for centuries.

The park's centerpiece is a trio of shimmering lakes, Lough Leane, Muckross Lake, and Upper Lake, all fed by the Killarney River's crystal-clear waters. These tranquil bodies of water, surrounded by ancient forests and towering mountains, create a serene and breathtaking environment that has long served as the inspiration for artists, poets, and nature lovers alike.

The majestic MacGillycuddy's Reeks, a rugged and imposing mountain range that serves as the backdrop to Killarney's breathtaking views, tower above the lakes. This dramatic landscape, with its craggy peaks and deep valleys, provides limitless opportunities for outdoor adventure, ranging from strenuous hikes to thrilling rock-climbing expeditions. But Killarney's geographical diversity goes beyond its lakes and mountains. The town also has a plethora of other natural wonders, such as ancient forests, cascading waterfalls, and lush meadows blooming with vibrant wildflowers. These diverse ecosystems support a diverse range of flora and fauna, including the iconic red deer, Ireland's only wild deer herd.

Killarney has a temperate oceanic climate, which is common throughout Ireland's southwestern region. This means that the town has mild temperatures all year, with average highs of around 18°C (64°F) in the summer and lows of about 6°C (43°F) in the winter.

One of the most notable aspects of Killarney's climate is its high precipitation, which contributes to the region's lush, verdant landscapes. The town gets an average of 1,400 mm (55 inches) of rain per year, with the wettest months being winter and early spring.

While this may deter some visitors, the intermittent showers and mist-shrouded landscapes add to the town's timeless enchantment.

CHAPTER 2

PLANNING YOUR TRIP

GETTING TO KILLARNEY

By plane. Kerry Airport (ORK) is the most convenient airport for visitors to Killarney, located only 15 kilometers from the town center. This regional airport has direct flights from several major European hubs, including London, Frankfurt, and Paris, making it an easily accessible entry point for international visitors. Upon arrival, you can easily arrange ground transportation, such as a taxi, shuttle service, or rental car, to complete your trip to Killarney.

Alternatively, you can fly into one of Ireland's larger international airports, such as Shannon Airport (SNN) or Cork Airport (ORK), which are about 90 minutes and 1.5 hours from Killarney, respectively. While these airports provide a wider range of flight options, you must account for the additional travel time and expense to reach your final destination.

By train. For those who prefer to travel by rail, Killarney is well connected to the Irish rail network, with regular services running from major cities nationwide. Killarney Railway Station is located in the heart of town, making it a convenient option for those who do not have transportation.

The most popular train route to Killarney departs from Dublin's Heuston Station, taking approximately 3.5 hours. Other major cities, such as Cork, Limerick, and Tralee, have direct train connections to Killarney, allowing you to take in the stunning Irish countryside on your way there.

Killarney is easily accessible by bus, with regular services connecting it to other cities and towns in Ireland. The main bus station, located in the town center, serves as a hub for both local and intercity routes, offering visitors a dependable and cost-effective transportation option. Several major bus companies, including Bus Éireann and Expressway, provide daily service to Killarney from Dublin, Cork, Limerick, and other major hubs. The journey time varies depending on the origin, but you can expect to arrive in Killarney in about 4-5 hours from Dublin and 1-2 hours from the surrounding cities.

By Car. For those who want the freedom and flexibility to explore the region at their own pace, renting a car is an excellent option. Killarney is easily accessible by road, with well-kept motorways and scenic country roads linking it to the rest of Ireland. If you plan to drive to Killarney, you should familiarize yourself with the local traffic laws and customs, as driving on the left side of the road may be unfamiliar to some international visitors. Additionally, be prepared for the region's narrow, winding streets, which can pose a unique challenge for those unfamiliar with Irish driving conditions.

Arriving in Killarney, regardless of mode of transportation, is a must-do on any Ireland travel itinerary. Whether you choose the ease of air travel, the romance of rail travel, the flexibility of a rental car, or the affordability of the bus, you will be rewarded with breathtaking natural landscapes, rich cultural experiences, and the warm hospitality of the Irish people.

VISA REQUIREMENTS

Travelling to the enchanting town of Killarney, Ireland necessitates careful consideration of the country's visa and entry requirements, which vary depending on your nationality and the purpose of your visit. Ireland, as a member of the European Union, has specific regulations in place to manage foreign nationals' entry, ensuring that all visitors have a smooth and secure travel experience. If you are a citizen of a European Union (EU) or European

Economic Area (EEA) member state, you are eligible to enter Ireland, including Killarney, without a visa. As part of the EU's free movement policy, EU/EEA citizens can freely travel, reside, and work within the borders of any member state, including Ireland, by presenting a valid national ID card or passport. Citizens of the following countries can enter without a visa: Austria, Belgium, Bulgaria, Croatia, Cyprus, Czechia, Denmark, Estonia, Finland, France, Germany, Greece, Hungary, Iceland, Ireland, Italy, Latvia, Liechtenstein, Lithuania, Luxembourg, Malta, the Netherlands, Norway, Poland, Portugal, Romania, Slovakia, Slovenia, Spain, Sweden, and Switzerland. For visitors who are not citizens of an EU or EEA member country, the visa requirements for entering Ireland, including Killarney, may differ depending on their nationality and the purpose of their visit.

Certain non-EU/EEA nationals are not required to obtain a visa for short-term visits to Ireland, including trips to Killarney. The following nationalities do not require a visa:
- USA.
- Canada.
- Australia.

- New Zealand.
- Japan.
- Singapore.
- South Korea

Travelers from these countries can enter Ireland without a visa for up to 90 days as long as they have a valid passport and can prove the reason for their visit, such as tourism, business, or visiting family and friends. Nationals from countries not on the visa-exempt list will need a valid visa to enter Ireland, including Killarney. The type of visa required depends on the purpose and length of your stay. The most popular visa options for travelers to Killarney are:

I. Schengen Visa (Short-Term Stay): Visitors from non-EU or non-EEA countries who are not visa-exempt may be required to obtain a short-stay Schengen visa before entering Ireland. This visa allows for stays of up to 90 days within 180 days and is appropriate for tourism, business, or visiting purposes.

II. Long Stay Visa (D-Visa): A long-stay D-visa may be required for visitors to Ireland, including Killarney, who intend to stay for more than 90 days. This type of visa is typically issued for purposes such as education, employment, or family reunification.

It is important to note that the visa application process can take several weeks, so plan your trip and submit your visa application on time. Depending on the type of visa you are applying for, you may also be required to provide additional supporting documents such as a valid passport, proof of accommodation, proof of financial means, and a detailed itinerary. Consult a reputable travel agency or the Irish embassy or consulate in your home country to ensure that you understand the specific visa requirements for your nationality and the purpose of your trip to Killarney, Ireland.

ACCOMMODATIONS FOR ANY BUDGET AND STYLE

When it comes to finding the ideal place to stay during your visit to the picturesque town of Killarney, Ireland, there are numerous and diverse options available to travelers of all budgets and preferences. Killarney has a wide range of accommodation options to ensure a comfortable and memorable stay, including luxurious hotels, cozy bed and breakfasts, self-catering apartments, and charming guesthouses.

Luxury Hotels: Killarney has several world-class luxury hotels that offer unrivaled service and amenities to those looking for the ultimate in elegance and pampering. These properties are ideal for special occasions, romantic getaways, or those who simply want to enjoy the finer things in life. The Killarney Park Hotel, a five-star establishment with beautifully landscaped grounds, is one of Killarney's most well-known luxury hotels. Guests can expect spacious, beautifully appointed rooms, a cutting-edge wellness center, fine dining restaurants, and the meticulous attention to detail that distinguishes the best hotels. Another high-end option is the Dunloe Hotel & Gardens, a stunning property nestled in the breathtaking scenery of the Gap of Dunloe. This grand hotel features opulent rooms, an award-winning spa, and a variety of dining options that highlight the region's renowned culinary heritage.

Boutique Hotels & Guesthouses: Killarney's boutique hotels and charming guesthouses offer a more intimate and personalized experience than large-scale accommodations.

These properties frequently feature one-of-a-kind, individually designed rooms, warm hospitality, and a strong connection to the local community. The Europe Hotel & Resort, for example, combines contemporary design with traditional Irish charm while providing breathtaking views of the nearby lakes and mountains.

The Killarney Plaza Hotel and Spa, on the other hand, is a beautifully restored 19th-century structure that has been transformed into a sophisticated yet cozy boutique retreat. Those seeking a truly authentic Irish experience may choose to stay at one of Killarney's family-run guesthouses, such as the Killaran House or the Dromhall Hotel. These establishments provide a warm, welcoming atmosphere, with delicious homemade breakfasts and personalized recommendations for exploring the surrounding area.

Self-catering Apartments and Cottages: Families, groups, and travelers looking for more independence and flexibility may find that self-catering accommodations, such as apartments and cottages, are ideal for their Killarney vacation. These types of accommodations offer the comforts of home, including kitchen facilities, living areas, and extra space, making them ideal for extended stays or those who prefer to cook for themselves. One popular option is Killarney Holiday Village, which has a variety of self-catering cottages and townhouses set in beautifully landscaped grounds just a short distance from the town center. Similarly, Fossa Holiday Homes offers modern, well-equipped apartments and houses ideal for families or groups looking to explore Killarney like a local.

Budget-Friendly Alternatives: For travelers on a tighter budget, Killarney still has plenty of affordable lodging options. From traditional bed and breakfasts to hostels and budget hotels, there are plenty of affordable options to meet the needs of every traveler. The Killarney Riverside Hotel, for example, provides comfortable, clean rooms at reasonable prices, whereas the Killarney International Hostel offers a social, eco-friendly environment for solo adventurers or backpackers.

Alternatively, the Eviston House Hotel offers excellent value while also being conveniently located in the heart of Killarney's vibrant town center. Killarney has something for everyone, regardless of their budget or preferred style of accommodation. By carefully researching and comparing the various options available, you can find the ideal place to stay while exploring this enchanting Irish town and its surrounding natural wonders.

WHEN TO VISIT

The picturesque town of Killarney, located in County Kerry, is a year-round destination that provides visitors with a diverse range of experiences. However, the best time to visit Killarney depends on your interests, travel preferences, and desired activities. From the lively summer months to the peaceful winter, this comprehensive guide will assist you in determining the best time to plan your trip to Killarney, Ireland.

Spring (March-May): Spring is a wonderful time to visit Killarney because the town and its surrounding landscapes come alive with the vibrant colors of blooming flowers and the gradual return of warm weather. Expect comfortable temperatures this season, with average highs ranging from 12°C (54°F) to 16°C (61°F). One of the highlights of a spring visit to Killarney is the chance to see the stunning transformation of the local flora.

The town's famous gardens, such as the Muckross House and Gardens, come to life with a kaleidoscope of daffodils, azaleas, and rhododendrons, creating an unforgettable visual spectacle. Furthermore, the Killarney National Park's lush, emerald-green landscapes are at their peak, providing picturesque hiking and sightseeing opportunities. Spring also brings a new energy to Killarney, with numerous local festivals and events taking place, including the Killarney St. Patrick's Day Parade and the Killarney Races. This is a great time to immerse yourself in the town's vibrant culture and traditions, as the local's welcome warmer weather and the promise of summer.

Summer (June-August): The summer months are unquestionably the busiest tourist season in Killarney, with visitors flocking to the town to take advantage of the warm, sunny weather and the abundance of outdoor activities available. The average temperature during this time ranges from 16°C (61°F) to 21°C (70°F), making it an excellent time to explore the town's numerous natural wonders. One of the main attractions of Killarney during the summer is the opportunity to visit the breathtaking Killarney National Park, which includes lakes, mountains, and ancient forests.

Visitors can go on scenic hikes, rent boats to explore the serene lakes, or simply enjoy the natural beauty of the area. Furthermore, the town's vibrant cultural scene is in full swing, with a busy calendar of festivals, concerts, and events, including the well-known Killarney Racing Festival. Summer is also the busiest season in Killarney, with the town's pubs, restaurants, and shops bustling with activity. It's an ideal time to immerse yourself in the local culture, sample the region's renowned cuisine, and enjoy the legendary Irish hospitality.

Autumn (September–November): As summer turns to autumn, Killarney becomes more serene and contemplative. The crowds thin out, and the town's natural beauty transforms as the trees' leaves change color, resulting in a stunning autumnal palette. During the autumn months, average temperatures in Killarney range from 10°C (50°F) to 16°C (61°F), making it ideal for outdoor activities that do not require extreme heat or bright sunlight. Visitors can take relaxing hikes through Killarney National Park, where the changing foliage and crisp, fresh air create a truly magical atmosphere. Autumn is also an excellent time to explore Killarney's rich cultural heritage, with fewer crowds allowing for more intimate encounters at the town's historical sites, including Muckross House, Dunloe Castle, and the famous Ross Castle. This season also brings an exciting calendar of local festivals, such as the Killarney Food & Music Festival and the Killarney Autumn Arts Festival, which provide a glimpse into the town's thriving arts and culinary scene.

Winter (December - February): While the winter months in Killarney can be cold, with average temperatures ranging from 5°C (41°F) to 10°C (50°F), the town transforms into a winter wonderland, providing a unique and enchanting travel experience. The rugged landscapes of Killarney National Park take on a serene, almost mystical quality, and the town transforms into a cozy, inviting haven for visitors.

One of the primary benefits of visiting Killarney during the winter is the opportunity to participate in the town's festive celebrations. The Christmas season in Killarney is especially magical, with twinkling lights, bustling Christmas markets, and the sounds of traditional Irish music and carols filling the air.

During the winter, visitors can enjoy a slower pace of life by exploring the town's charming shops, galleries, and cozy pubs, where they can sample the region's renowned cuisine and friendly service. Furthermore, fewer visitors allow for more intimate experiences, such as guided tours of Killarney's historical sites and private activities like horse-drawn carriage rides through the peaceful countryside.

Killarney provides visitors with a one-of-a-kind and memorable travel experience year-round. By taking into account your interests and travel preferences, you can schedule the ideal visit to this enchanting Irish town and create lasting memories of your time on the Emerald Isle.

ESSENTIAL PACKAGING LIST

Given Killarney's temperate maritime climate, you should pack a versatile wardrobe that can adapt to changing weather conditions. Begin with a foundation of comfortable, breathable layers like t-shirts, long-sleeved tops, and lightweight sweaters or cardigans. Bring a variety of pants, including lightweight options for warm days and heavier trousers or jeans for colder weather. A high-quality, waterproof jacket is essential, as the region is prone to sudden rain showers. Look for a jacket with a hood to keep you dry and comfortable even in the harshest weather. Don't forget to bring a warm hat, gloves, and scarf, as temperatures can drop, particularly during the shoulder and winter seasons. When it comes to footwear, make comfort your priority. Invest in a reliable pair of walking shoes or boots with good traction, as you will most likely be doing a lot of exploring on foot. Consider bringing a second, more casual pair of shoes for evening outings or less strenuous activities.

To fully enjoy Killarney's stunning natural landscapes, pack the necessary outdoor gear. A sturdy, well-fitting backpack or daypack will be necessary for transporting your essentials on hikes and outdoor adventures. Don't forget to pack water bottles, snacks, and any necessary medications. If you plan on hiking in Killarney National Park, make sure to bring a good pair of hiking socks and gaiters to keep your feet and lower legs dry and protected. Trekking poles can be extremely useful for navigating the region's uneven terrain.

For water-based activities like boating or kayaking, bring quick-drying clothing, water shoes, and a lightweight, packable raincoat or poncho.

If you're a photographer, make sure to bring your camera, lenses, and any other equipment you'll need to capture the breathtaking scenery. In addition to clothing and outdoor gear, your Killarney packing list should include a few practical items. Make sure you include the following:

- Chargers and adapters for your electronics.
- A power bank or portable charger to keep your gadgets charged.
- A reusable water bottle or thermos.
- Sunscreen, lip balm.
- Insect repellent.
- First-aid kit containing necessary medications.
- Travel documents (passport, identification, travel insurance, etc.).
- A small sum of local currency (euros) for incidentals and tips.
- Killarney guidebook or maps.
- Notebook and pen to take notes and make recommendations

Packing the essentials on this comprehensive list will ensure that you are well-prepared for your Killarney adventure, regardless of the weather or activities you have planned.

CHAPTER 3

GETTING AROUND KILLARNEY

PUBLIC TRANSPORTATION

Killarney's primary mode of public transportation is the bus system, which is operated by Bus Éireann, the national provider. The town's main bus station, located in the heart of the city center, serves as a hub for both local and intercity routes, connecting Killarney to destinations across County Kerry and beyond. Killarney has several local bus routes that connect the town to key landmarks, neighborhoods, and amenities. These routes are especially useful for visitors who want to explore the town without relying on their transportation. Some of the most popular local bus routes are:

- o Route 270 connects the town center to Killarney National Park, which includes popular attractions such as Muckross House and the Gap of Dunloe.
- o Route 271 connects the town center to the Killarney Railway Station, making it convenient for train passengers.
- o Route 272 connects Killarney's residential areas, hospitals, and educational institutions.

In addition to the local bus network, Killarney is well connected to other towns and cities in Ireland via Bus

Éireann's intercity bus services. These routes provide direct connections to major hubs such as Dublin, Cork, Limerick, and Tralee, allowing visitors to easily explore the surrounding region during their stay. Some of the most popular intercity bus routes serving Killarney are:

Dublin to Killarney: With multiple daily departures, this route connects Killarney to Ireland's capital city, taking approximately 4.5 hours.

Cork to Killarney: This route connects Killarney to the vibrant city of Cork, with buses running frequently and the trip lasting approximately 1.5 hours.

Limerick to Killarney: Travelers can easily reach Killarney from Limerick via bus, which takes approximately 1.5 hours.

For those looking for a more direct and personalized mode of transportation, Killarney has a dependable taxi network. Taxis can be hailed directly from the town's main taxi rank, which is near the bus station, or pre-booked through local taxi companies. Taxis in Killarney are especially useful for short trips around town, as well as transfers to and from the nearby Kerry Airport or other transportation hubs. Fares are metered, and drivers are generally knowledgeable about the surrounding area, making them an easy choice for visitors.

Killarney's compact size and picturesque landscapes make it an ideal place to explore by bicycle. The town has several bicycle rental shops, allowing visitors to explore the town and surrounding natural wonders on two wheels. Renting a bicycle is an excellent way to explore Killarney National Park, which has a vast network of cycling trails and paths. It also allows you to explore charming neighborhoods, historic sites, and scenic viewpoints at your leisure, free from the constraints of public transportation schedules.

RENTING A CAR

Exploring the enchanting town of Killarney and its surrounding region is unquestionably enhanced by the freedom and flexibility of having your rental car. Renting a car in Killarney allows you to explore the area's breathtaking natural beauty, charming villages, and hidden gems at your leisure, free from the constraints of public transportation schedules or tour group itineraries. As you prepare for your Killarney adventure, familiarize yourself with the car rental process and local driving customs to ensure a smooth and enjoyable experience. This comprehensive guide will walk you through the main considerations and steps for renting a car in Killarney, Ireland.

Renting a car is a popular and recommended way to explore Killarney and the surrounding County Kerry area. With a rental car, you can plan your itinerary, make spontaneous stops, and explore the area's hidden gems. Killarney National Park, with its stunning lakes, mountains, and historic sites, is ideal for self-driving because it allows you to freely navigate scenic routes and stop at lookout points and trailheads as you see fit.

A rental car also allows you to take day trips to nearby towns and attractions, such as the stunning Ring of Kerry or the breathtaking Dingle Peninsula, without having to coordinate public transportation. Killarney is well served by a variety of rental car companies, giving visitors plenty of options and competition. Some of the major car rental companies with locations in Killarney are:

- o   Hertz.
- o   Avis.

- Enterprise.
- Europcar.
- Sixt.

These companies have offices conveniently located throughout town, often near the Killarney train station or the town center, making it simple to pick up and drop off your rental vehicle. When researching and booking your rental car, make sure to compare prices, vehicle options, and any additional fees or policies between providers to find the best deal for your needs and budget. Driving in Killarney and throughout Ireland can be a unique experience for visitors, particularly those who are used to driving on the right side of the road. Here are some essential tips to remember:

- Drive on the left side of the street.
- Be familiar with roundabouts and yield to traffic that is already in the circle.
- Exercise caution on narrow, winding roads, especially in rural areas.
- Follow all traffic signs and speed limits.
- Keep to the left when driving and passing other vehicles.

- Exercise extra caution when navigating steep hills and hairpin turns.
- Be aware of livestock and farmers on country roads.

It is also necessary to obtain an International Driving Permit (IDP) or ensure that your home country's driver's license is valid in Ireland. This will help to avoid problems when renting and driving a vehicle during your stay. When renting a car in Killarney, you should carefully consider the insurance and coverage options available to protect both yourself and the vehicle.

Most rental companies provide various types of insurance, such as collision damage waiver (CDW), theft protection, and liability coverage. It is critical to carefully read the rental agreement and understand what is and is not covered by the rental company's insurance policies. You should also check with your personal auto insurance provider or credit card company to see if they provide coverage for rental cars, as this could save you money on additional insurance. By taking the time to plan and prepare for a car rental in Killarney, you'll be well on your way to an unforgettable and seamless exploration of Ireland's most enchanting region.

With the freedom and flexibility of your vehicle, you can create a truly unique travel experience, discovering the hidden gems and breathtaking landscapes that make Killarney and the Emerald Isle so appealing.

CYCLING

Killarney, located in the heart of Ireland's breathtaking southwest, is known for its stunning natural landscapes and endless opportunities for outdoor adventure. Bicycling is one of the most exciting and rewarding ways to experience Killarney's beauty, as it allows you to immerse yourself in the region's picturesque scenery, discover hidden gems, and connect with the local culture at your leisure. Whether you're a seasoned cyclist or a beginner, Killarney has something for everyone, with a wealth of meticulously maintained trails, scenic routes, and bike-friendly infrastructure to ensure a safe and memorable adventure.

Killarney's cycling scene revolves around the renowned Killarney National Park, a 26,000-hectare expanse of pristine wilderness that provides some of Ireland's most scenic and diverse cycling experiences. The park's network of well-marked trails and roads is a cyclist's dream, allowing you to discover the breathtaking lakes, mountains, and ancient forests that have captivated visitors for centuries.

The "Muckross Lake Loop," a 14-kilometer circuit through the park's most iconic landscapes, includes the historic Muckross House, the tranquil Muckross Lake, and the enchanting Torc Waterfall. Along the way, you'll see breathtaking views, spot local wildlife, and learn about Killarney's rich cultural heritage. For those looking for a more challenging experience, the park includes several steep climbs and technical descents that will put even the most experienced cyclists to the test. The Gap of Dunloe, a dramatic mountain pass that cuts through the Macgillycuddy's Reeks range, is a standout, providing a thrilling and visually stunning ride for those up to the challenge.

Beyond the boundaries of Killarney National Park, the town is an excellent starting point for exploring the renowned Ring of Kerry, a scenic driving route that follows the stunning coastal landscapes of the Iveragh Peninsula. While the Ring of Kerry is traditionally traveled by car, it has also become a popular destination for cyclists, who can enjoy a truly immersive and unforgettable experience of the region's natural beauty.

Cycling the Ring of Kerry is a difficult but rewarding endeavor, covering a total distance of approximately 179 kilometers (111 miles) and a wide range of terrain, from flat coastal roads to steep, winding mountain passes. The route leads you through quaint seaside villages, past ancient stone monuments, and along the dramatic cliffs and beaches that have made this part of Ireland famous. For those looking for a more manageable cycling experience, there are numerous options to tackle sections of the Ring of Kerry, allowing you to create your itinerary and focus on the areas that most interest you. Local tour operators and bike rental shops can offer valuable advice and assistance, ensuring that your cycling trip around the Ring of Kerry is safe, enjoyable, and tailored to your abilities.

Killarney's thriving cycling community has resulted in an abundance of bike rental and support services to meet the needs of both casual and avid cyclists. Visitors can easily rent high-quality bicycles, ranging from sleek road bikes to sturdy mountain bikes and e-bikes, from a variety of reputable shops throughout town. In addition to bike rentals, these local businesses provide a variety of support services such as guided tours, shuttle transfers, and even luggage transportation, ensuring that your cycling trip in Killarney is smooth and stress-free. Many shops also offer detailed route maps, recommendations, and emergency assistance, allowing cyclists of all skill levels to easily navigate the region's extensive network of trails and roads.

WALKING TOURS

One of the best ways to fully immerse yourself in Killarney's charm and character is to go on a walking tour, which will allow you to discover the town's hidden gems and gain a better understanding of its rich story tapestry. From guided tours led by knowledgeable local experts to self-guided explorations, Killarney has a wide range of walking experiences to suit all traveler's interests and abilities.

Whether you want to take a stroll through the town's bustling streets, a strenuous hike in Killarney National Park, or an in-depth look at the area's cultural and historical significance, there's a walking tour for you.

Guided Walking Tours: For those looking for a more structured and informative experience, Killarney's guided walking tours are an excellent choice. These tours, led by passionate, knowledgeable guides, provide a wealth of insights and anecdotes that bring the town's history and culture alive. The Killarney Historical Walking Tour is a popular guided tour that takes visitors through the town's fascinating history. This tour explores the architectural, religious, and political influences that have shaped Killarney over the centuries, visiting highlights such as Killarney Cathedral, the Killarney Court House, and the iconic Ross Castle.

Another interesting option is the Killarney Leprechaun and Folklore Walking Tour, which combines the town's rich mythological history with its breathtaking natural beauty. Guests will learn about the mischievous leprechauns, fairies, and other legendary creatures that are said to live in Killarney National Park while exploring the park's tranquil lakes, ancient forests, and picturesque scenery. The Killarney Food Tour offers a more specialized experience, taking participants on a culinary adventure through the town's vibrant food scene, sampling local delicacies from artisanal producers, family-run cafes, and traditional pubs. This tour provides a delicious opportunity to discover the flavors that define Killarney's distinct culinary identity.

Self-guided Walking Trails: In addition to guided tours, Killarney provides a network of well-marked, self-guided walking trails that allow visitors to explore the town and its surrounding natural wonders at their leisure. These trails accommodate a variety of fitness levels and interests, making them accessible to people of all ages and abilities.

The Killarney Town Walking Trail is one of the most well-known self-guided experiences, taking visitors on a stroll through the town center, highlighting the town's historic buildings, lively pubs, and charming local shops. Along the way, informative signage and maps provide context and insights, allowing you to create your unique exploration. For those looking for a more challenging outdoor adventure, the Killarney National Park Walking Trails provide a variety of routes that showcase the park's diverse landscapes, ranging from serene lakes and ancient woodlands to majestic mountain peaks. Whether you choose the Dinis Cottage Trail, the Torc Waterfall Trail, or the Gap of Dunloe, each self-guided walk promises breathtaking scenery and a deeper connection to nature.

Specialized Walking Tours: Aside from the town's standard walking experiences, Killarney also provides a variety of more specialized tours that cater to specific interests and perspectives. For example, the Killarney Ghostly Walking Tour invites brave souls to explore the town's supernatural side, uncovering spine-tingling legends passed down through generations. Meanwhile, the Killarney Literary Tour takes visitors on a journey through the lives and works of famous Irish writers and poets who have been inspired by the town's breathtaking landscapes.

Whatever your preferred pace or area of interest, Killarney's walking tours offer an unrivaled opportunity to discover the heart and soul of this enchanting Irish town. Whether you join a guided group or embark on your own self-guided adventure, you'll come away with a greater appreciation for Killarney's rich history, vibrant culture, and breathtaking natural beauty.

CHAPTER 4
EATING AND DRINKING IN KILLARNEY

TRADITIONAL IRISH CUISINE

Killarney, located in the heart of Ireland's picturesque County Kerry, has long been known for its rich culinary heritage, which is deeply rooted in the region's abundant natural resources and Irish traditions. From fresh seafood plucked from the nearby Atlantic Ocean to hearty, comforting dishes passed down through generations of Killarney residents, the town's gastronomic landscape offers a diverse and delectable exploration of the Emerald Isle's most beloved flavors.

At the heart of Killarney's traditional cuisine is a deep respect for the land and a dedication to using the freshest, locally sourced ingredients. The town's proximity to the Atlantic coast, fertile agricultural regions, and abundant natural resources of Killarney National Park provides a wealth of high-quality, seasonal produce, which serves as the foundation of the local culinary scene. Seafood is a celebrated staple, with the town's restaurants and pubs serving up a variety of freshly caught delicacies ranging from succulent Atlantic salmon and tender white fish to the iconic Irish staple, the mighty Atlantic oyster. These briny delights are frequently prepared using simple yet masterful techniques, allowing the natural flavors to shine. Aside from the bounty of the sea, Killarney's culinary traditions rely heavily on the fertile farmlands that surround the town. Local dairy products, such as rich, creamy cheeses and the well-known Irish butter, are essential in both savory and sweet recipes. Similarly, the region's pasture-raised livestock, such as beef, lamb, and pork, are highlighted in hearty stews, roasts, and sausages that have stood the test of time.

While Killarney's culinary landscape has evolved to incorporate modern gastronomic trends, the town's traditional home-cooked dishes remain at the heart of its cuisine. These time-honored recipes passed down through generations, provide a warm and comforting taste of Ireland's vibrant cultural heritage. The iconic Irish stew, a slow-simmered medley of tender lamb, potatoes, onions, and aromatic herbs that embodies the very essence of Irish comfort food, is one of Killarney's most representative traditional dishes.

Another popular dish is the Irish breakfast, which consists of grilled sausages, rashers (Irish bacon), black and white puddings, eggs, and soda bread. Beyond these celebrated staples, Killarney's culinary traditions include a variety of hearty, rustic dishes that highlight the town's agricultural bounty. Shepherd's pie, with its fluffy mashed potato topping and savory minced lamb filling, is a perennial favorite, as is the hearty Irish casserole, which combines meat, vegetables, and savory broth.

While Killarney's culinary reputation is founded on its savory specialties, the town also has a long history of sweet treats and desserts that have delighted generations of locals and visitors alike. One of Killarney's most famous delicacies is traditional Irish soda bread, a dense, crumbly quick bread with a distinct texture thanks to the use of baking soda as a leavening agent. This versatile staple can be eaten on its own, topped with Irish butter, or used as the foundation for a variety of sweet and savory recipes.

For those with a sweet tooth, Killarney offers an array of indulgent confections, from buttery, flaky shortbread cookies known as "Irish biscuits" to decadent, cream-filled pastries known as "rock buns." Killarney's skilled bakers also put their unique spin on classic desserts, such as the creamy, dreamy Irish coffee trifle and the rich, indulgent Guinness cake. As you explore Killarney's culinary landscape, you'll discover that each bite, sip, and morsel tell a story about the town's deep connection to the land, the sea, and the enduring traditions that have sustained its people for generations.

RESTAURANTS

Traditional Irish pubs. Killarney is known for its vibrant pub culture, and these establishments frequently serve as the heart and soul of the community, providing much more than just a place to grab a pint. Many of the town's traditional Irish pubs also serve delicious home-cooked meals that highlight the best of Irish cuisine. One such establishment is the Laurels Pub, which is located in Killarney's town center.

For generations, this cozy, family-run pub has served both locals and visitors, offering a menu of hearty stews, homemade bread, and classic dishes like shepherd's pie and fish and chips. The Laurels is also known for its lively music sessions, where local musicians come together to perform traditional Irish songs. The Dunloe Bar is another well-known Killarney pub, located at the base of the majestic

McGillycuddy's Reeks Mountain range. This charming establishment not only provides a warm and welcoming atmosphere, but also houses a well-known restaurant that serves fresh seafood, tender steaks, and other Irish favorites. The Dunloe Bar is a popular spot for those looking to experience the town's vibrant pub culture while eating a delicious, locally sourced meal.

Fine dining establishments: While traditional Irish pubs are a must-see on any Killarney trip, the town also has a growing number of fine dining establishments that are making waves in the culinary scene. These upscale restaurants highlight Ireland's celebrated produce, seafood, and culinary traditions, often with a modern twist. One such establishment is the Bricin Restaurant, which is housed within the historic Bricin Building. This award-winning restaurant serves a seasonally inspired menu that highlights the bounty of County Kerry, with dishes featuring locally sourced ingredients like fresh Atlantic seafood, grass-fed Irish beef, and organic produce. The Bricin's elegant yet welcoming atmosphere and impeccable service make it a popular choice for special occasions and unforgettable dining experiences.

The Porterhouse Restaurant, located inside the luxurious Killarney Park Hotel, is another high-end dining option in Killarney. This fine dining establishment has breathtaking views of the town's lush, green landscapes and serves a menu that combines the best of Irish and international culinary traditions. From expertly prepared steaks and seafood to inventive vegetarian and vegan dishes, the Porterhouse Restaurant is a must-see for those looking for a truly exceptional dining experience.

Casual Dining and Cafés: In addition to the town's traditional pubs and high-end restaurants, Killarney offers a diverse range of casual dining options and charming cafés to suit a variety of budgets and dietary needs. The Handsome Burger, a modern burger joint that uses high-quality, locally sourced ingredients to put a gourmet spin on the classic hamburger, is a popular place for a relaxing meal. This casual eatery is popular with both locals and visitors, thanks to its lively and welcoming atmosphere and delicious menu. Killarney has a thriving café culture, with places like the Cappuccino Bar and the Killarney Brewing Company Taproom serving expertly crafted coffee, tea, and a selection of homemade baked goods and light bites.

When dining out in Killarney, it's important to understand the local tipping customs and etiquette. In Ireland, a tip of 10-15% of the total bill is customary for table service in restaurants, pubs, and cafés. However, it's always a good idea to check the menu or ask your server, as some restaurants may include a service charge in the final bill. It's also worth noting that "splitting the bill" is less common in Ireland than it is in other countries.

When dining in a group, it is generally expected that the bill will be settled collectively, with each person contributing their share. Killarney's restaurants and eateries are well-versed in meeting a variety of dietary needs and food allergies. Whether you have specific dietary requirements or simply want to sample the local cuisine, most establishments will gladly assist you in finding appropriate menu options or providing alternative preparations to accommodate your preferences.

When making reservations or ordering, make sure to communicate any dietary restrictions or allergies to your server so that they can guide you through the menu and ensure a safe and enjoyable dining experience.

LOCAL SPECIALTIES

Seafood Specialties: Killarney's location on the stunning Wild Atlantic Way ensures an abundance of fresh, high-quality seafood. From the crystal-clear lakes and rivers to the rugged Atlantic coastline, the region's waters are teeming with delicious marine life, which is celebrated in the town's vibrant culinary scene.

One of Killarney's most recognizable local specialties is the renowned Kerry Lamb, which is prized for its exceptional flavor and tenderness. These lambs graze on the Iveragh Peninsula's lush, nutrient-rich grasses, producing meat of unparalleled richness and depth of flavor. Visitors can try a variety of Kerry Lamb dishes, from hearty stews and roasts to creative preparations that highlight the meat's versatility.

Dairy delights: The rolling green pastures and lush farmlands of County Kerry also support a thriving dairy industry, which has produced some of Ireland's most celebrated artisanal cheese and dairy products. Killarney is a hotspot for these delectable treats, with local cheesemakers and creameries proudly displaying their products in the town's markets, shops, and restaurants.

One of the most notable local specialties in this category is the renowned Dingle Peninsula Cheeses, which include the award-winning Cashel Blue and the creamy, soft-ripened Knockalara. These cheeses, made with traditional methods and the region's high-quality milk, are frequently served with local breads, chutneys, and preserves for a truly harmonious flavor experience.

Similarly, Killarney is home to several well-known ice cream producers who use the area's exceptional dairy products to create premium, artisanal ice creams in a variety of traditional and innovative flavors. These frozen treats, which range from classic Irish cream to unique seasonal offerings, are a must-try for any visitor with a sweet tooth.

Traditional Irish fare: Of course, no culinary tour of Killarney would be complete without sampling the town's extensive selection of traditional Irish dishes and comfort foods. These time-honored recipes passed down through generations, highlight the hearty, wholesome nature of Irish cuisine, frequently incorporating locally sourced ingredients and traditional cooking methods. One such local specialty is the well-known Irish Stew, a slow-cooked, fragrant dish made with lamb or beef, potatoes, onions, and a variety of aromatic herbs and spices. This comforting meal is a popular choice in Killarney's pubs and restaurants, offering a warm and satisfying taste of the town's culinary heritage. Another traditional Irish dish is Soda Bread, a simple but delicious quick-baked loaf that goes well with everything from soups and stews to cheese platters and breakfast spreads. Killarney's artisanal bakers take great pride in their soda bread recipes, which frequently incorporate local ingredients such as buttermilk, raisins, or caraway seeds to create a unique twist on a timeless classic.

Locally Distilled Spirits: No visit to Killarney's culinary scene would be complete without a taste of the town's renowned locally distilled spirits. The Emerald Isle has long been known for its exceptional whiskeys, gins, and liqueurs, and Killarney is home to several renowned distilleries that are pushing the boundaries of traditional Irish spirits. One such local specialty is the iconic Dingle Whiskey, a smooth and complex single malt made with traditional methods and the Dingle Peninsula's pure, mineral-rich waters. Visitors can learn about the art of whiskey-making firsthand by touring the Dingle Distillery and tasting the various expressions of this celebrated spirit. Similarly, Killarney is home to several award-winning gin distilleries, including Skellig Six18 Distillery, which creates a line of innovative, botanically-infused gins that highlight the region's distinct terroir. These spirits often served with premium tonics and local garnishes, are a refreshing and sophisticated way to experience Killarney's vibrant drink culture.

Whether you're a foodie looking for an authentic taste of Ireland or a traveler simply looking to sample the local cuisine, Killarney's diverse selection of local specialties is sure to leave an impression. From the town's exceptional seafood and dairy products to its traditional Irish dishes and innovative spirits, this charming destination is a sensory delight, providing visitors with access to the best of Ireland's celebrated culinary heritage.

CHAPTER 5

TOP ATTRACTIONS IN KILLARNEY

KILLARNEY NATIONAL PARK

Killarney National Park, Ireland's crown jewel, is a must-see for any visitor to the region. This lush, picturesque landscape stretches over 102 square kilometers and is a true haven for nature lovers, providing an unparalleled opportunity to immerse yourself in the breathtaking beauty of the Emerald Isle.

The Killarney National Park, known for its breathtaking lakes, mountains, and ancient forests, is a veritable treasure trove of natural wonders, each more captivating than the last. Whether you're looking for a peaceful hike, a scenic boat tour, or simply a chance to reconnect with nature, this incredible park has something for people of all ages and interests.

When you enter Killarney National Park, you'll be struck by the sheer scale and grandeur of the scenery. The park is home to three magnificent lakes: Lough Leane, Muckross Lake, and Upper Lake, each with its distinct charm and character. Towering mountains, such as Macgillycuddy's Reeks and Killarney's highest peak, Carrauntoohil, provide a magnificent backdrop for your adventures.

In addition to the breathtaking natural scenery, Killarney National Park is known for its rich cultural heritage. The park contains several historic sites and attractions, including the stunning Muckross House, a 19th-century Victorian mansion that provides insight into the aristocratic way of life of the time. The park also includes ancient monasteries, picturesque villages, and a wealth of archaeological treasures, giving visitors a better understanding of Ireland's fascinating history. To protect the delicate ecosystem and ensure the safety of all visitors, Killarney National Park has established a set of rules and regulations that must be followed. This includes:

- Follow designated trails and pathways to minimize environmental impact.
- Avoid disturbing or removing wildlife, plants, or geological features.
- Keep your pet on a leash at all times.
- Dispose of all waste properly in the designated bins.
- Respect the park's peace, and avoid making loud noises or engaging in disruptive behavior.
- Follow all instructions and guidelines issued by park rangers and staff.

Killarney National Park, with its vast array of natural and cultural attractions, provides visitors with a wealth of activities and experiences to enjoy. Some of the best things to see and do in the park include:

I. Hiking and Trekking: Discover the park's vast network of hiking trails, which range from easy, accessible routes to more difficult, strenuous treks. Don't pass up the opportunity to hike to the summit of Ireland's highest mountain, Carrauntoohil.

II. Boat Tours: Take a tranquil boat tour of the park's beautiful lakes, which provide a unique perspective on the surrounding landscapes and wildlife.

III. Cycling: Rent a bicycle and explore the park's well-kept cycling trails, which will allow you to cover more ground and discover hidden gems.

IV. Horse-Drawn Carriage Rides: Take in the park's enchanting beauty from the comfort of a traditional horse-drawn carriage, a romantic and leisurely way to explore the area.

V. Cultural Attractions: Learn about the park's rich cultural heritage by visiting the Muckross House and Gardens, the Killarney House and Gardens, and the ancient Ross Castle.

VI. Wildlife Watching: Keep an eye out for the park's diverse flora and fauna, which includes red deer, native Irish red squirrels, and several bird species.

Killarney National Park is open all year, with varying hours and accessibility based on the season. The park is generally open from 8:00 a.m. to 6:00 p.m. during the peak summer months, while winter hours may be reduced to 9:00 a.m. to 4:30 p.m. The park's main visitor centers, located in Killarney and at the Muckross House, provide a wealth of information, maps, and directions to help you plan your visit. Many of the park's trails and attractions are wheelchair accessible, making it an ideal destination for people of all abilities.

MUCKROSS HOUSE AND GARDENS

Killarney, a premier travel destination in Ireland's picturesque southwest, is well-known for its breathtaking natural beauty and rich cultural heritage. The magnificent Muckross House and Gardens, located in the heart of this enchanting setting, is one of the area's most well-known attractions. This grand 19th-century mansion, surrounded by the breathtaking landscapes of Killarney National Park, provides visitors with a truly immersive experience, transporting them to a bygone era and offering a glimpse into the lives of Ireland's aristocratic past.

Muckross House, built in the Tudor style, is a Victorian architectural masterpiece, complete with ornate stonework, intricate woodcarvings, and elegant furnishings that have been meticulously preserved over the years. The Herbert family, whose lineage dates back to the 12th century, commissioned the stately manor, which was completed in 1843. Today, the house is a museum, where visitors can explore its opulent interiors and learn about the fascinating history that occurred within its walls.

Guided tours of the Muckross House take visitors through the property's 65 rooms, which include the grand drawing rooms, the ornate dining hall, and the well-appointed chambers, all of which have been faithfully restored to their former glory. Along the way, knowledgeable guides tell fascinating stories about the house's original inhabitants, Victorian social customs, and Muckross' significant role in the development of Killarney National Park.

The magnificent Muckross House is surrounded by breathtaking gardens that have been meticulously cultivated and maintained over the centuries. The Muckross Gardens, which cover more than 30 hectares, are a true botanical paradise, with a stunning collection of rare and exotic plant species from all over the world. Visitors can explore a variety of themed gardens, each providing a distinct horticultural experience.

The Sunken Garden, with its vibrant blooms and soothing water features, is a standout, as is the elegant Rose Garden, which boasts an impressive collection of over 3,000 rose bushes. The Arboretum, on the other hand, has an impressive collection of towering trees from around the world, creating a serene and shaded oasis for visitors to explore. Beyond the formal gardens, the Muckross grounds include a network of walking trails that wind through Killarney National Park, providing breathtaking views of the surrounding lakes and mountains. Visitors can take strolls, spotting native wildlife and admiring the stunning natural beauty that has made this part of Ireland so famous. To preserve this historical and environmental treasure, visitors to Muckross House and Gardens are expected to follow a few simple rules and guidelines:

- Show respect for the property and its contents by not touching or handling any artifacts or furnishings.
- Stick to designated paths and trails; do not enter any restricted or private areas.
- Keep noise to a minimum, especially inside the house, to avoid disturbing other visitors.
- Dispose of all waste properly in the designated receptacles and refrain from littering.
- Leashed pets are allowed in the gardens but not in the house.

Muckross House and Gardens are open to the public year-round, except for a few special holidays. During the peak tourist season (April to October), the house and gardens are open daily from 9:00 a.m. to 5:30 p.m., with admission ending at 5:00 p.m. Winter hours (November to March) are slightly reduced, with the property open from 9:00 a.m. to

4:30 p.m. and the last admission at 4:00 p.m. Visitors should budget at least 2-3 hours to fully explore the house, gardens, and surrounding trails. The Muckross House offers guided tours regularly, with the first tour starting at 9:30 a.m. Tickets can be purchased on-site or, for a more convenient experience, in advance via the property's official website or authorized third-party vendors. Muckross House and Gardens, one of Killarney's most iconic and well-preserved historical attractions, provides visitors with a one-of-a-kind opportunity to step back in time and immerse themselves in Ireland's rich cultural tapestry.

TORC WATERFALL

The Torc Waterfall, one of Killarney's premier natural wonders, is a true gem that no traveler should miss while visiting this enchanting corner of Ireland. Nestled within the breathtaking Killarney National Park, this magnificent cascading waterfall provides the ideal combination of natural beauty, serene tranquility, and a glimpse into the region's rich history. Torc Waterfall is conveniently located just 6 kilometers from Killarney's town center, making it an easily accessible tourist attraction.

The most popular and recommended route to the waterfall is via the scenic Torc Waterfall Trail, a well-marked hiking path that winds through the park's lush forests and landscapes. The Torc Waterfall Trail trailhead is located just off the N71 road, with plenty of parking available in the designated car park. The waterfall is a simple 2-kilometer (1.2-mile) hike from the parking lot that takes about 30-45 minutes each way, depending on your pace and fitness level. Alternatively, for those who prefer a more leisurely pace or have mobility issues, a shuttle bus service is available during peak tourist season, transporting visitors directly to the waterfall's viewing platform.

As you approach the Torc Waterfall, the sound of cascading water will gradually become louder, creating a sense of anticipation and excitement. The waterfall itself is impressive, plunging 18 meters (59 feet) over a rocky outcrop to create a dramatic, thunderous display. When you reach the main viewing platform, you will be able to appreciate the waterfall's full grandeur, including its powerful flow and the lush, verdant surroundings that frame it. The platform offers excellent photographic opportunities and allows visitors to appreciate the waterfall's sheer size and beauty. For those who want a closer look, a series of steps lead down to the waterfall's base, where you can feel the mist on your face and fully immerse yourself in the sights and sounds of this natural wonder. However, it is important to note that the steps can be quite steep and slippery, so proceed with caution, particularly in wet conditions. Torc Waterfall is located within Killarney National Park, a protected natural area, so visitors must follow a few rules and regulations to preserve the site's integrity:

- Always stay on the designated paths and trails, and avoid going off-trail or scrambling on rocks.
- Do not climb on or near the waterfall; this is extremely dangerous and strictly prohibited.
- Keep noise to a minimum to maintain the site's serene atmosphere.
- Properly dispose of all litter and waste in the designated bins provided.
- Pets are allowed but must be kept on a short leash at all times.

The Torc Waterfall is open all year, with the peak tourist season typically occurring from late spring to early autumn

(April to September). During these months, the waterfall is usually at its most impressive, with abundant water flow and lush, vibrant vegetation all around it. However, the waterfall can be enjoyed throughout the year, as each season has its distinct charm. The waterfall's flow may be reduced in the winter, but the surrounding landscape takes on a serene, almost mystical quality, with snow-capped peaks in the distance.

The Torc Waterfall Trail and viewing platforms are open daily from dawn to dusk, with no set opening or closing times. It's important to note that the trail may be temporarily closed or have restricted access due to weather or maintenance work, so make sure to check for any updates or alerts before visiting.

While the Torc Waterfall is undoubtedly the main attraction for many visitors, it is only one of the many natural wonders to be discovered in the breathtaking Killarney National Park. After admiring the waterfall, consider visiting the park's other attractions, including the picturesque lakes, the historic Muckross House and Gardens, and the famous Gap of Dunloe.

ROSS CASTLE

The magnificent Ross Castle, one of Killarney's most iconic and well-preserved landmarks, is a must-see destination for any traveler exploring Ireland's breathtaking natural beauty in the southwest. This captivating 15th-century castle, nestled on the shores of Lough Leane, provides visitors with a one-of-a-kind glimpse into Killarney's rich history and cultural heritage, as well as breathtaking views that will leave an impression.

Ross Castle dates back to the late 15th century when it was built as a stronghold for the O'Donoghue clan, a powerful Gaelic family that ruled the surrounding lands. Over the centuries, the castle has seen numerous sieges, battles, and ownership changes, making it a testament to Ireland's turbulent history.

Today, Ross Castle is a beautifully preserved example of a traditional Irish stronghold, complete with imposing stone walls, circular towers, and a stunning lakeside setting. The castle's strategic location, overlooking the tranquil Lough Leane, made it an important defensive structure, and it helped shape the history of the Killarney region.

As you approach the castle, you'll notice its impressive size and the attention to detail in its architecture, which combines Gothic and Renaissance elements. Visitors can explore the castle's interior, which has been painstakingly restored to provide insight into the lives of its former occupants. During your visit, you will be able to wander through the castle's grand halls, climb the spiral staircases to the upper floors, and admire the breathtaking views of the surrounding landscape from the castle's towers. The property also includes a lovely walled garden, which provides a peaceful escape from the hustle and bustle of the main castle.

One of the highlights of visiting Ross Castle is the opportunity to take a traditional boat tour of Lough Leane, which departs directly from the castle's jetty. These leisurely boat rides provide a unique perspective on the castle as well as the opportunity to appreciate the stunning natural beauty of Killarney National Park. To protect this historical treasure, Ross Castle has a few rules and regulations in place for visitors:

Admission Fees: There is a fee to enter the castle, which can be paid on-site or online in advance. Seniors, students, and children can take advantage of discounted rates.

Photography: Photography is generally permitted throughout the castle, but tripods and flash photography may be prohibited in certain areas.

Accessibility: Although the castle's interior is accessible, some areas may have limited access due to the building's historical significance. Visitors with mobility issues are encouraged to inquire about accessibility options upon arrival.

Tour Times: The castle is open to the public at specific times, which vary depending on the season. It is recommended that you check the castle's website or inquire about the current schedule upon arrival.

Guided Tours: Visitors can take a guided tour of the castle to learn more about its history and features. These tours are scheduled at specific times throughout the day.

Ross Castle is open to the public year-round, with slightly reduced hours in the winter. During the peak season (April to October), the castle is typically open from 9:30 AM to 5:30 PM, and from 10:00 AM to 4:00 PM during the off-season (November to March).

It's worth noting that the castle may be closed on certain holidays or for special events, so visitors should check the castle's website or contact the on-site staff for the most recent information.

As previously stated, the castle's interior is generally accessible, with ramps and gentle inclines to assist visitors with mobility issues. Due to the building's historic nature, some areas, such as the upper floors and towers, may be inaccessible. Visitors with special needs should inquire about accessibility options upon arrival or when planning their visit.

GAP IN DUNLOE

The Gap of Dunloe, carved out by glacial erosion over thousands of years, is a stunning example of the powerful forces that shaped Ireland's landscape. As you travel along the narrow, winding road, you will be surrounded by towering, jagged peaks that rise to 1,000 meters (3,280 feet) on either side, creating a dramatic and otherworldly atmosphere. The road, which is only accessible to pedestrians, horse-drawn jaunting cars, and bicycles, winds through the valley, allowing visitors to immerse themselves in the area's natural beauty and tranquility. Along the way, you'll see several glacial lakes, including the breathtaking Kate Kearney's Cottage, which is a popular starting point for many visitors. The Gap of Dunloe is a treasure trove of natural and cultural attractions, providing visitors with a wide range of opportunities to explore and discover.

I. Hiking and Walking: The Gap of Dunloe is a hiker's paradise, with numerous well-marked trails and paths winding through the valley. Whether you choose a stroll or a more strenuous hike, you will be rewarded with breathtaking views and the opportunity to immerse yourself in the region's rugged natural beauty.

II. Jaunting Car Rides: One of the most iconic and traditional ways to explore the Gap of Dunloe is to take a jaunting car ride. These horse-drawn carts, driven by locals, provide a unique and scenic way to explore the valley while also revealing the region's rich cultural heritage.

III. Boating on the Lakes: The Gap of Dunloe's series of glacial lakes, including the famous Black Lake, offers the opportunity for a peaceful and picturesque boat ride.

Visitors can take a boat tour and enjoy the tranquil waters and surrounding mountain scenery.

IV. Fishing: The lakes and streams in the Gap of Dunloe are well-known for their excellent trout and salmon fishing opportunities. Visitors with a valid fishing license can try their hand at casting a line while enjoying the tranquil surroundings.

V. Picnicking and Photography: The Gap of Dunloe is a photographer's paradise, with countless opportunities to capture the valley's breathtaking natural beauty. Visitors can also enjoy a picnic while taking in the breathtaking scenery and sounds of this enchanting location.

The Gap of Dunloe is open year-round and accessible to pedestrians, horse-drawn vehicles, and bicycles. The best time to visit is during the warm months when the weather is more conducive to outdoor activities. Visitors can park at Kate Kearney's Cottage, a popular starting point for Gap of Dunloe activities. From there, you can explore the valley on foot, by car, or by taking a boat tour. Dress appropriately for your visit to the Gap of Dunloe, as the weather in Ireland can be unpredictable. Wear comfortable, weatherproof clothing and sturdy, closed-toe shoes, and prepare for potentially wet and windy weather.

The Gap of Dunloe is a protected natural area with rules and regulations to preserve its delicate ecosystem. Visitors are expected to follow designated paths, avoid littering, and respect the local wildlife and vegetation. Pets are generally permitted but must be kept on a leash. The Gap of Dunloe has limited dining options, but nearby Beaufort and Killarney offer a variety of restaurants, pubs, and other amenities to meet visitor needs. As you travel through the breathtaking landscapes of the Gap of Dunloe, you will be transported to a world of unspoiled natural beauty, rich cultural heritage, and limitless opportunities for exploration and adventure.

RING OF KERRY

The breathtaking Ring of Kerry, located in southwestern Ireland, is one of the country's most iconic and popular tourist attractions. This scenic coastal route, which spans 170 kilometers (105 miles) through County Kerry's stunning landscapes, provides travelers with an unforgettable experience, showcasing the best that the Emerald Isle has to offer.

The Ring of Kerry, which winds through a tapestry of rugged cliffs, golden beaches, picturesque villages, and lush, rolling hills, is a sensory feast. As you travel along this captivating loop, you will be treated to breathtaking views that have inspired artists, poets, and adventurers for generations. The route passes through some of Ireland's most breathtaking natural wonders, including the iconic Killarney National Park, the dramatic Skellig Islands, and the quaint coastal towns of Kenmare, Sneem, and Waterville. Each stop along the way provides a one-of-a-kind and enchanting experience, inviting visitors to immerse themselves in the region's rich cultural heritage, outdoor activities, and natural beauty.

The Ring of Kerry is a treasure trove of attractions and experiences that cater to a diverse range of interests and preferences. Here are some of the best highlights and must-do activities along the way:

I. Killarney National Park: Discover the lush forests, glistening lakes, and historic estates that comprise this breathtaking national park. Visitors can go hiking, cycling, horseback riding, or take a traditional jaunting car tour.

II. Skellig Islands: Take a boat tour to the breathtaking Skellig Islands, a UNESCO World Heritage Site that once housed a monastery but is now a haven for seabirds, including the iconic puffin.

III. Muckross House and Gardens: Explore this beautifully preserved 19th-century mansion and its exquisite gardens, which provide insight into the region's aristocratic past.

IV. Dingle Peninsula: Depart from the main Ring of Kerry route and explore the Dingle Peninsula, which is known for its charming fishing villages, rugged coastline, and the iconic Dingle Way hiking trail.

V. Fishing and Watersports: The Ring of Kerry's numerous rivers, lakes, and coastal areas provide ideal conditions for fishing, kayaking, and other water-related activities.

VI. Culture and Crafts: Visit local artisanal workshops, traditional Irish pubs, and heritage sites to learn about the region's history and traditions.

VII. Scenic Drives and Photography: The Ring of Kerry is a photographer's dream, with countless opportunities to capture breathtaking landscapes ranging from dramatic cliffs to serene lakes and charming villages.

Driving the Ring of Kerry allows you to explore the sights and attractions at your own pace. The route can be driven in either direction, but the most popular direction is clockwise, beginning in Killarney. The Ring of Kerry offers ample parking and facilities, including visitor centers, restrooms, and picnic areas. It is recommended that you plan your stops and check for available parking ahead of time, particularly during peak tourist seasons.

Depending on your interests and stops, the Ring of Kerry loop can take 4-8 hours to complete. It is best to allow enough time to fully immerse yourself in the experience without feeling rushed. Dress in layers and bring appropriate clothing and footwear for the Ring of Kerry's unpredictable weather and outdoor activities. Sturdy walking shoes, weatherproof jackets, and sunscreen are all recommended.

The Ring of Kerry is a protected natural and cultural heritage area with rules and regulations in place to preserve the environment and ensure visitor safety. Travelers are expected to follow designated paths, avoid littering, and respect the local wildlife and vegetation. The Ring of Kerry is an unforgettable jewel in Killarney's crown. Setting out on the captivating journey along the Ring of Kerry is a truly transformative experience that will leave an indelible impression on all who embark. From the breathtaking natural landscapes to the rich cultural heritage and warm hospitality of the locals, this iconic route provides a comprehensive and immersive exploration of Killarney and the surrounding region's best offerings

THE SKELLIG ISLANDS

Perched on the edge of the Atlantic Ocean off Ireland's southwest coast, the Skellig Islands are a testament to the Emerald Isle's rugged beauty and captivating history. These remote, rocky outposts, designated as a UNESCO World Heritage Site, have long captivated travelers, scholars, and adventurers alike, providing a glimpse into a bygone era and an opportunity to connect with the natural wonders that have shaped this remarkable region.

The larger of the two Skellig Islands, Skellig Michael, is the true jewel in the crown, with profound historical significance and unparalleled natural beauty. This dramatic, craggy island, which rises 230 meters (755 feet) above the crashing waves, was once home to a thriving monastic community that sought solace and spiritual enlightenment in the remote, windswept confines of this outpost. The monastery's well-preserved remains, dating from the sixth century, demonstrate the resilience and ingenuity of these early Christian settlers.

Visitors can explore the intricate beehive-shaped huts, the unique stone stairways, and the ancient oratory while admiring the breathtaking natural landscapes that surround them. Skellig Michael's importance in the history of early Christianity is highlighted by its designation as a UNESCO World Heritage Site, which recognizes the island's profound cultural and archaeological significance. While the larger Skellig Michael receives a lot of attention, the smaller, uninhabited island of Little Skellig is equally captivating. This rugged limestone outcrop supports one of the world's largest gannet colonies, with over 30,000 pairs nesting on its cliffs. Visitors can marvel at the sheer number of gannets, as well as other seabird species like puffins, kittiwakes, and razorbills, who have all made the Little Skellig their home. The island's inaccessibility and protected status have allowed these bird populations to flourish, making it a true ornithological treasure trove.

Access to the Skellig Islands is strictly controlled, with visitors required to book a boat tour in advance to ensure the preservation of the fragile ecosystem and the safety of all who visit these remote outposts. Boat tours to the Skellig Islands depart from Portmagee and other designated launch points on the Kerry coast. The boat ride itself can be difficult, as the waters around the islands can be rough and unpredictable, especially during the off-season.

The Skellig Islands are a protected natural and cultural heritage site. Visitors must follow strict guidelines and regulations to preserve the environment and ensure their safety. This includes a daily visitor limit, mandatory guides, and strict protocols for accessing the island and its historical sites.

The Skellig Islands offer breathtaking natural beauty and historical significance, making them a must-see destination. Skellig Michael's highlights include well-preserved monastic ruins, ancient stone stairways, and breathtaking coastal views. The opportunity to see the thriving gannet colony on Little Skellig is a must-see for birdwatchers and nature enthusiasts.

The Skellig Islands provide hiking trails and guided tours for adventurous travelers to explore the natural and cultural wonders of the islands. However, it is important to note that these activities are physically demanding and should only be attempted by those with adequate fitness levels and equipment.

Visiting the Skellig Islands requires careful planning and preparation. Visitors should expect unpredictable weather, difficult terrain, and limited amenities on the islands themselves. Appropriate clothing, sturdy footwear, and provisions for the boat ride and stay on the islands are required.

The Skellig Islands are a testament to nature's enduring power and human resilience. These remote, awe-inspiring outposts, with their rich history, captivating natural beauty, and distinct wildlife, have captured the hearts and minds of travelers for centuries.

KILLARNEY LAKES

The Killarney Lakes are the focal point of the renowned Killarney National Park, a UNESCO Biosphere Reserve with a wide range of landscapes, from rugged mountain peaks to lush, ancient forests. As you explore this captivating natural wonderland, you'll be treated to a sensory feast, with each of the three lakes having its distinct charm and character.

The Upper Lake, with its serene, mirror-like surface and surrounding hills, is a true oasis of calm, ideal for a peaceful boat ride or a stroll along the shoreline. The Middle Lake, flanked by the majestic McGillycuddy's Reeks Mountain range, is a stunning sight, with its waters reflecting the dramatic, jagged peaks that tower overhead. The Lower Lake, with its picturesque islands and historic landmarks, is a hub of activity, providing numerous opportunities for exploration and discovery. The Killarney Lakes are a haven for outdoor enthusiasts, with a wide range of activities and experiences available to visitors of all interests and skill levels.

I. Boating and Water Sports: Visitors can explore the lakes in a traditional rowing boat, kayak, or on a guided boat tour, immersing themselves in the tranquil waters and taking in the breathtaking scenery.

II. Hiking and Walking Trails: Killarney National Park has a vast network of hiking trails that wind through the lakes and surrounding forests, providing opportunities to discover hidden gems and take in the region's natural beauty.

III. Fishing: The lakes are well-known for their excellent fishing opportunities, where anglers can try their hand at catching trout, salmon, and other freshwater species.

IV. Birdwatching: The Killarney Lakes and their surrounding habitats support a diverse range of birdlife, including the iconic red deer, making it a birdwatcher's paradise.

V. Historic Sites and Landmarks: Visitors can learn about the region's rich cultural heritage by visiting the iconic Ross Castle, the imposing Muckross House, and the ancient monastic ruins scattered throughout the landscape.

The Killarney Lakes are easily accessible from Killarney town, with multiple access points and parking facilities located throughout the national park. Visitors can explore the lakes by foot, boat, or using the park's extensive network of roads and trails. Killarney National Park, including its lakes, is open year-round, with peak season from May to September. Before scheduling a visit, visitors should check for any seasonal closures or changes in operating hours. Killarney National Park and its lakes follow strict rules and regulations to preserve the fragile ecosystem. Visitors are expected to follow designated paths, avoid littering, and respect the local wildlife and vegetation.

The Killarney National Park provides visitor facilities such as restrooms, picnic areas, and refreshment stands. Visitors are encouraged to bring their supplies, as amenities may be limited in more remote areas of the park. To prepare for the unpredictable weather and outdoor activities at Killarney

Lakes, visitors should dress in layers and wear sturdy, comfortable footwear. It is also recommended that they bring sun protection, rain gear, and any equipment required for the activities they intend to undertake.

JAUNTING CARS

The jaunting car in Killarney dates back to the nineteenth century when wealthy landowners and aristocratic visitors used horse-drawn carriages for transportation and leisure. Over time, the jaunting car became a beloved part of local culture, with skilled drivers, known as "jarveys," sharing their extensive knowledge of the region's history and natural wonders with each passenger.

Today, the jaunting car is an essential part of the Killarney experience, providing a tangible link to the area's storied past and demonstrating the enduring traditions that continue to shape this captivating corner of Ireland. Stepping into a jaunting car is like traveling back in time, as you settle into the comfortable, wooden carriage and embark on a guided tour through the breathtaking landscapes of Killarney National Park and the surrounding countryside.

I. The Gap of Dunloe: One of the most popular scenic driving routes takes visitors through the dramatic, glacier-carved valley of the Gap of Dunloe, which provides breathtaking views of the majestic MacGillycuddy's Reeks Mountain range.

II. Killarney Lakes: Jaunting car tours frequently include stops at the serene and picturesque Killarney Lakes, where you can admire the sparkling waters and historic landmarks along the shoreline.

III. Muckross Estate: Many jaunting car tours include a visit to the Muckross Estate, a beautifully preserved 19th-century mansion, and gardens that provide insight into the region's aristocratic history.

IV. Customized Experiences: Some jaunting car operators provide more personalized tours, allowing visitors to create their itineraries and explore the areas that are most interesting to them.

Jaunting car tours in Killarney are a truly unique and memorable experience, allowing visitors to immerse themselves in the region's rich history and natural beauty while traveling in a leisurely, old-world mode of transportation. The jaunting car drivers, also known as "jarveys," are local experts with extensive knowledge of the area's history and geography. They take great pride in their job and are often eager to share their experiences and insights with passengers. The horses that pull the jaunting cars are well-cared for and accustomed to Killarney's winding roads and trails.

Jaunting cars are built for comfort, with padded seats and plenty of legroom. While the ride is generally smooth and relaxing, visitors should expect some minor bumps and jolts as the carriage negotiates the uneven terrain. Safety is a top priority, and all jaunting car operators follow stringent regulations and safety protocols. Jaunting car tours typically last 30 minutes to several hours, depending on the route and level of customization. Pricing varies depending on the operator and the length of the tour, but it typically starts around €10-15 per person for a simple, short excursion.

Jaunting car tours are extremely popular, particularly during the peak tourist season. It is recommended that you book your tour in advance to ensure your preferred date and time.

Many operators provide online booking options to make the process easier. A jaunting car tour in Killarney is a truly enchanting experience, allowing visitors to step back in time and immerse themselves in the region's rich cultural heritage and breathtaking natural beauty, which have defined it for centuries. Whether you're exploring the dramatic landscapes of the Gap of Dunloe, admiring the serene Killarney Lakes, or discovering the historic Muckross Estate, the jaunting car provides a one-of-a-kind and unforgettable way to connect with Killarney's essence and the enduring traditions that continue to captivate visitors from all over the world.

CHAPTER 6

ACTIVITIES IN KILLARNEY

HIKING AND WALKING TRAILS

Killarney, located in the heart of County Kerry, is renowned as one of Ireland's top destinations for outdoor enthusiasts and nature lovers. Killarney's breathtaking landscapes, picturesque lakes, and ancient forests provide an unparalleled variety of hiking and walking trails to suit a wide range of skill levels and interests. Whether you're looking for a relaxing stroll, a strenuous hike, or an immersive exploration of the region's rich cultural heritage, Killarney's trails promise an unforgettable adventure.

The Killarney National Park, a UNESCO Biosphere Reserve with a breathtaking array of natural wonders, is central to Killarney's hiking and walking offerings. The national park, which covers over 26,000 hectares, is home to a vast network of trails that wind through a tapestry of ancient oak forests, tranquil lakes, and majestic mountain peaks.

One of the park's most popular trails, the Muckross Lake Trail is a moderate 11-kilometer (7-mile) loop that leads hikers past the iconic Muckross House, along the shores of the stunning Muckross Lake, and through the tranquil Oakwoods.

Torc Waterfall Trail is a 4.5-kilometer (2.8-mile) loop trail which takes visitors to the breathtaking Torc Waterfall, a 20-meter (65-foot) cascade that flows over a series of rocky steps. The trail provides panoramic views and opportunities to observe native wildlife. For those looking for a more difficult hike, the Cardiac Hill trail, which is part of the longer Mangerton Mountain trek, offers a steep ascent to the summit and rewards hikers with panoramic views of the Killarney Valley and the surrounding McGillycuddy's Reeks Mountain range.

The Kerry Way, which extends far beyond the boundaries of Killarney National Park, is a well-known long-distance hiking trail that winds through County Kerry's breathtaking landscapes. This iconic route spans over 200 kilometers (124 miles) and provides a comprehensive exploration of the region's natural and cultural wonders.

The Dingle Way is a section of the Kerry Way that takes hikers on a fascinating journey along the rugged Dingle Peninsula, highlighting the region's dramatic coastline, charming villages, and ancient archaeological sites. Another section of the Kerry Way, the Beara Way provides a more difficult but equally rewarding experience, with winding trails through the Caha Mountains and along the dramatic Beara Peninsula. Killarney's hiking and walking trails are suitable for a variety of skill levels, from gentle, family-friendly strolls to more demanding, strenuous treks. Before embarking on a trail, visitors should research its specifics and difficulty levels to ensure they are prepared for the physical demands.

Killarney's mild, temperate climate allows for year-round hiking, with the summer months (May to September) being the most popular and accessible. Visitors should be prepared for changing weather conditions, including appropriate clothing and gear because Ireland's weather is unpredictable. The main trailheads for Killarney's hiking routes are located in Killarney National Park, which has several access points and parking facilities. Visitors should check for seasonal closures or restrictions before planning their hikes.

Killarney offers a variety of organized hiking tours led by knowledgeable local guides who can provide information about the region's history, ecology, and hidden gems. Furthermore, Killarney and the surrounding area have a diverse range of accommodation options to suit all budgets and preferences. As a protected natural area, Killarney National Park and the Kerry Way trail system have strict rules and regulations in place to protect the fragile ecosystems. Visitors are expected to stay on designated paths, clean up any litter, and respect the local wildlife and vegetation. The hiking and walking trails in Killarney, Ireland, provide a truly transformative experience, allowing visitors to immerse themselves in the region's breathtaking natural beauty, rich cultural heritage, and fascinating history.

CYCLING ROUTES

Killarney's cycling routes offer a truly unique and unforgettable way to experience the best that this magnificent region has to offer. Whether you're drawn to the rugged coastal vistas of the Ring of Kerry, the serene tranquility of the Killarney Lakes, or the challenging ascents of the McGillycuddy's Reeks Mountain range, the cycling opportunities in and around Killarney are as diverse as they are stunning. As you pedal your way through the winding roads and picturesque byways, you'll be treated to a symphony of sights, sounds, and experiences that will leave a lasting impression on your memory. Discover historic landmarks like the iconic Ross Castle and the stately Muckross House while passing through charming villages that showcase Ireland's rich cultural heritage. Marvel at the dramatic cliffs and golden beaches that line the coastline, and feel a deep connection with the natural world as you climb through lush, verdant forests and ascend to breathtaking panoramic views. Killarney's cycling network is extensive and well-developed, accommodating a wide range of abilities and preferences. Here are some of the must-see cycling routes and trails that visitors can take:

I. The Ring of Kerry Cycle: This 179-kilometer (111-mile) loop is the pinnacle of Killarney's cycling offerings, highlighting the region's breathtaking coastal landscapes, charming villages, and historic landmarks. The route is difficult but rewarding, with both flat stretches and difficult climbs.

II. The Killarney National Park Cycle: This scenic route winds through the heart of Killarney National Park, providing an opportunity to immerse yourself in the region's natural wonders, such as the captivating Killarney Lakes and the majestic McGillycuddy's Reeks.

III. The Dingle Peninsula Cycle: Depart from the main Ring of Kerry route and explore the rugged beauty of the Dingle Peninsula, which includes dramatic cliffs, charming fishing villages, and the iconic Slea Head Drive.

IV. The Kerry Way Cycle: This long-distance cycling trail follows the famous Kerry Way hiking trail, providing a more peaceful and serene alternative to the busy Ring of Kerry. It's ideal for those who want a more remote and off-the-beaten-path experience.

V. The Beara Peninsula Cycle: Located on County Kerry's southern coast, the Beara Peninsula is a lesser-known gem that offers breathtaking coastal scenery, picturesque villages, and an unparalleled sense of tranquility.

Killarney is well-equipped to meet the needs of cyclists, with a vast network of bike lanes, designated cycling routes, and a variety of bike rental and repair services available throughout the area.

As with any cycling destination, visitors must follow local traffic regulations, wear appropriate safety gear, and use caution when sharing the road with other vehicles. Killarney's roads can be narrow and winding, so cyclists should exercise extreme caution. Killarney's cycling routes offer a variety of terrain, ranging from relatively flat and easy to difficult climbs and technical descents. Cyclists should choose a route that is appropriate for their skill level and physical fitness.

Proper planning is essential for a successful and enjoyable cycling trip in Killarney. Visitors should bring the necessary equipment, including a well-maintained bicycle, appropriate cycling attire, and essential tools and supplies for repairs and hydration. Cycling in Killarney can be seamlessly combined with a variety of other activities and attractions, including hiking, boating, cultural experiences, and culinary delights.

Visitors are encouraged to discover the region's diverse offerings and plan their trips accordingly. Cycling through the breathtaking landscapes of Killarney, Ireland, is a transformative experience that allows visitors to connect with the Emerald Isle on a deeply personal level.

GOLFING

Killarney has an impressive collection of golf courses, each with its distinct charm and set of challenges for players of all skill levels. The region caters to the diverse preferences and abilities of its golfing guests, offering championship-caliber layouts as well as more accessible, family-friendly options.

The renowned Killarney Golf & Fishing Club is the jewel of Killarney's golfing offerings, with three stunning championship courses: Killarney National Park, Mahony's Point, and Killeen. These meticulously maintained layouts, designed by renowned golf architects, provide a true test of skill, with each course offering its own unique set of captivating features and strategic challenges.

The Killarney National Park course, in particular, is a true masterpiece that winds through the breathtaking scenery of Killarney National Park. Golfers are treated to breathtaking views of the majestic McGillycuddy's Reeks Mountain range and the tranquil lakes that dot the landscape, making for an unforgettable golfing experience. Numerous other golf courses in the Killarney region, such as the Dooks Golf Club and the Beaufort Golf Club, provide equally impressive settings and well-designed layouts, catering to golfers of all preferences.

Killarney's golf courses are complemented by a wide range of amenities and facilities designed to meet the needs of golfers. Luxurious clubhouses, pro shops stocked with the latest equipment and apparel, and on-site dining options ensure that visitors have a full golf experience. Many of the courses also provide excellent practice facilities, such as driving ranges, chipping greens, and putting greens, allowing golfers to hone their skills before taking on the challenging layouts.

To improve the golfing experience in Killarney, local providers provide a variety of tailored packages and experiences that cater to visitors' various needs and preferences. Golfers can create their ideal golfing getaway by selecting from custom-designed tours and lessons with PGA-certified professionals, as well as luxury accommodations and dining packages. Killarney's comprehensive offerings make it an ideal destination for both individual golfers and groups, ensuring that every aspect of the experience is carefully planned and executed.

While the golf courses are unquestionably the main draw, Killarney has a plethora of other attractions and activities for visitors to enjoy during their stay. There are numerous opportunities to explore and discover the region's rich cultural heritage, as well as the stunning natural landscapes of Killarney National Park. Visitors can go on scenic hikes, participate in water sports on the lakes, or explore the charming towns and villages scattered throughout the countryside. The area's exceptional dining scene, which focuses on locally sourced ingredients and traditional Irish cuisine, enhances the overall experience.

Killarney's long-standing reputation as a golfer's paradise is well-deserved, given its captivating courses, world-class facilities, and breathtaking natural setting. Whether you're a seasoned golfer looking for a new challenge or a beginner looking to hone your skills in a breathtaking setting, Killarney provides an unforgettable golfing experience that will leave a lasting impression.

As you tee off in the sweeping vistas of Killarney National Park or putt your way to victory on the pristine greens of Killarney Golf & Fishing Club, you'll be captivated by the seamless integration of golf and nature - a true testament to the enduring allure of this golfing gem in the heart of Ireland.

WATER ACTIVITIES

At the heart of Killarney's water-based offerings are the enchanting Killarney Lakes, a three-lake system that has long captivated the hearts and imaginations of visitors from all over the world. These tranquil, mirror-like waters, framed by the majestic McGillycuddy's Reeks Mountain range, provide numerous opportunities for aquatic exploration and relaxation. Visitors can explore the lakes in traditional rowing boats, kayaks, or guided boat tours, immersing themselves in the tranquil beauty of their surroundings while discovering hidden coves, historic landmarks, and vibrant wildlife.

Anglers will have plenty of opportunities to cast a line and try their hand at catching trout, salmon, and other freshwater fish. Beyond the lakes, Killarney National Park has a network of rivers and streams that are equally appealing to water enthusiasts. Visitors can try their hand at fly fishing, canoeing, or kayaking through the gentle currents, or even go wild swimming in the park's natural swimming holes and plunge pools. Killarney's aquatic offerings extend beyond the lakeshores to the nearby Ring of Kerry coastline, which is rugged and dramatic. This scenic coastal route, known for its breathtaking views and ancient heritage sites, also provides a plethora of water-based activities for the daring traveler.

One of the most thrilling coastal experiences in Killarney is a visit to the Skellig Islands, a UNESCO World Heritage Site with a thriving seabird colony and the well-preserved ruins of an ancient Christian monastery. Visitors can take boat tours to these remote, rocky outposts to see the towering cliffs and the breathtaking sight of thousands of gannets, puffins, and other seabirds in their natural environment.

For those looking for a more hands-on aquatic adventure, the Ring of Kerry provides excellent opportunities for sea kayaking, which allows visitors to navigate the rugged coastline while spotting diverse marine life and discovering hidden coves and sea caves along the way. Reservations are required for many water-based activities in Killarney, including boat tours, kayak rentals, and guided fishing excursions, to ensure availability and quality experiences.

Visitors are encouraged to plan their trips and make reservations in advance, especially during peak tourist seasons. Killarney's aquatic activities follow strict safety regulations to protect all participants. Visitors should follow their guides' instructions, wear appropriate safety equipment, and be aware of any weather or water conditions that may affect their activities.

The availability and conditions of Killarney's water-based activities vary throughout the year, with the peak season lasting from late spring to early autumn. Before planning a trip, visitors should check for seasonal changes or closures. Killarney provides various amenities for water enthusiasts, such as equipment rental shops, launch sites, and refreshment stands. Visitors are encouraged to bring any necessary equipment, but should also be aware of the resources available in the surrounding area.

HORSE RIDING

Horseback riding has been an important part of Killarney's cultural fabric for centuries, with local stables and riding schools carrying on the time-honored traditions of this popular pastime.

The region's history is inextricably linked to the horse, with the iconic jaunting cars (horse-drawn carriages) serving as a popular mode of transportation for generations of visitors. Today, Killarney's equestrian scene is thriving, with a diverse range of riding experiences to suit everyone from seasoned equestrians to complete beginners. Whether you want to take a leisurely trail ride through the scenic countryside, participate in a thrilling cross-country excursion, or even learn the fundamentals of horseback riding, Killarney has the perfect equine adventure for your interests and skill level.

The opportunity to explore the breathtaking Killarney National Park from the saddle is unquestionably the highlight of Killarney's horseback riding offerings. This UNESCO Biosphere Reserve, with its lush forests, sparkling lakes, and majestic mountain peaks, provides a breathtaking natural playground for horse enthusiasts, allowing them to immerse themselves in the region's unspoiled beauty and rich cultural heritage. Guided trail rides through the national park are a popular option, allowing visitors to explore a network of well-kept paths and trails while taking in the sights and sounds of this fascinating landscape.

Experienced riders may even be able to take on more adventurous excursions, tackling difficult terrain and navigating the park's rugged landscapes. Regardless of the route or activity, a horseback adventure through Killarney National Park is sure to be an unforgettable experience, allowing visitors to connect with the land, the horses, and the region's enduring equestrian traditions. While Killarney National Park is unquestionably the highlight, the surrounding areas of County Kerry also provide a plethora of exciting horse-riding opportunities for visitors to discover.

Riders can enjoy exhilarating coastal rides, galloping across expansive sandy beaches and navigating the rugged cliff trails that hug the shoreline. These excursions not only offer an exhilarating equestrian experience but also breathtaking panoramic views of the Atlantic Ocean and the region's stunning seaside scenery. Killarney also has several cross-country riding facilities where riders can put their skills to the test and enjoy the rush of navigating obstacles and challenging terrain. These specialized venues cater to a wide range of skill levels, from beginner to advanced, allowing riders of all abilities to experience the thrill of cross-country riding in a safe and controlled setting. Killarney's horse-riding scene is supported by a network of high-quality stables, riding schools, and experienced equestrian professionals who are all committed to giving visitors an unforgettable experience. These facilities have well-trained, well-cared-for horses, as well as a team of knowledgeable instructors and guides who are eager to share their love of horses and the surrounding landscape.

Whether you're a seasoned rider or a complete beginner, you can be confident that you'll be in capable hands, receiving expert guidance and instruction tailored to your specific needs and abilities.

Many of these equestrian centers also provide a variety of additional services and amenities, including tack shops, farrier services, and the option to book multi-day riding packages, allowing visitors to fully immerse themselves in Killarney's equestrian lifestyle. A visit to Killarney, Ireland, is incomplete without experiencing the region's rich equestrian heritage and the exciting opportunities it provides for horse enthusiasts.

TRADITIONAL IRISH MUSIC AND DANCE

Killarney is well-known as a center for the preservation and celebration of traditional Irish music, with a thriving community of musicians, singers, and fans dedicated to keeping the age-old tunes and melodies alive and well. From the lively rhythms of the bodhrán (Irish frame drum) to the soulful melodies of the uilleann pipes, Killarney's music exemplifies the enduring power of this ancient art form.

Visitors to Killarney can immerse themselves in the vibrant musical culture by attending lively sessions in the town's traditional pubs, where local musicians gather to share their skills. These informal gatherings are the true highlight of any visit, providing a glimpse into the intimate, communal nature of traditional Irish music.

Listeners can feel the musicians' infectious energy as they weave intricate melodies and driving rhythms, transporting them to a world of pure, unadulterated joy. Aside from the pubs, Killarney has a full calendar of music festivals and events that honor the region's musical heritage. The Killarney Folk and Traditional Music Festival and Killarney Races Summer Music Series showcase traditional Irish music, including haunting sean-nós (unaccompanied singing) and exhilarating céilí band tunes.

Killarney's rich musical heritage is complemented by the captivating world of traditional Irish dance, a centuries-old art form that has come to represent the Emerald Isle's cultural identity. Killarney's dance scene revolves around the iconic Irish step dancers, whose intricate, rhythmic footwork and disciplined, upright posture has captivated audiences all over the world. Visitors can see these dancers' breathtaking artistry at local dance performances, which highlight the distinct styles and regional variations that have evolved over generations.

Killarney's dance traditions extend beyond the stage, with vibrant céilí dances held in community halls and local pubs. These lively gatherings allow visitors to immerse themselves in the social and communal aspects of traditional Irish dance, as both locals and tourists work together to master the intricate steps and formations. For the more daring, Killarney also offers traditional dance workshops and classes, where experienced instructors reveal the secrets of these captivating art forms.

Whether you're an experienced dancer or a complete beginner, these interactive experiences provide a one-of-a-kind and unforgettable opportunity to connect with the heart and soul of Killarney's cultural heritage.

Killarney's traditional music and dance provide visitors with an immersive and transformative experience, allowing them to form a deep and intimate connection to the Emerald Isle's rich cultural tapestry. From lively pub sessions to electrifying dance performances, these timeless art forms can transport the audience while stirring the soul and igniting the spirit.

As you learn about Killarney's musical and dance traditions, you will be welcomed into a warm, vibrant community that is fiercely proud of its heritage and eager to share its treasures with the rest of the world. Whether you're tapping your feet to the beat of a bodhrán or admiring the grace and athleticism of the step dancers, you'll leave with a renewed appreciation for the enduring power of these ancient art forms and a desire to return to this enchanting corner of Ireland.

CHAPTER 7

SHOPPING IN KILLARNEY

SOUVENIRS

Killarney has long been known for its rich traditions and skilled artisans, and this heritage is reflected in the region's timeless souvenirs.

I. Handcrafted Knitwear: Irish wool has long been prized for its exceptional quality and warmth, and Killarney's local knitwear shops offer a diverse selection of handcrafted sweaters, scarves, and accessories that highlight the intricate skills of the area's talented weavers.

II. Claddagh Rings: The iconic Claddagh ring, with its distinctive design of two hands clasping a crowned heart, is a traditional Irish symbol of love, friendship, and loyalty. These beautifully crafted rings are available in a variety of styles and materials, making them a timeless and meaningful souvenir.

III. Handmade Lace: Killarney's delicate, intricate lacework has been admired for centuries, and visitors can find a wide range of exquisite lace products, from doilies and tablecloths to fine art and jewelry.

IV. Aran Sweaters: The iconic Aran sweater, with its intricate cable knit patterns, is a popular Irish staple that has come to represent the country's rich cultural heritage. Killarney's artisanal knitters provide a variety of these timeless garments, ideal for staying warm during the Emerald Isle's cooler months.

While traditional Irish crafts remain popular souvenirs, Killarney's creative community has embraced modern, locally inspired designs that capture the essence of the region in new and innovative ways.

I. Artisanal Ceramics: Local potters and ceramicists have created a stunning collection of mugs, plates, and decorative pieces featuring distinctive Killarney-themed motifs, such as the town's iconic lakes and mountains and historic landmarks.

II. Handcrafted Jewelry: Killarney's talented jewelry makers have turned the region's natural beauty into wearable art, creating one-of-a-kind necklaces, earrings, and bracelets with local gemstones, metals, and designs.

III. Bespoke Leather Goods: The town's skilled leather artisans have created a collection of high-quality bags, wallets, and accessories that combine traditional leatherworking techniques with modern, Killarney-inspired designs.

IV. Artisanal Spirits and Liqueurs: Killarney's local distilleries and breweries offer a tempting selection of artisanal spirits, liqueurs, and beers that capture the essence of the region's rich agricultural heritage, making them ideal souvenirs.

As more visitors seek ethical and sustainable shopping experiences, Killarney's souvenir offerings have evolved to meet this growing demand. Many of the town's artisanal producers prioritize using locally sourced, environmentally friendly materials, as well as fair-trade and sustainable production methods. Visitors can be proud that their souvenir purchases not only celebrate Killarney's unique character but also benefit the local economy and skilled craftspeople. A souvenir-hunting adventure in Killarney is a truly immersive experience, allowing visitors to connect with the town's rich cultural heritage, vibrant creative community, and natural wonders that have inspired generations of artists. Whether you're drawn to the timeless allure of traditional Irish crafts or the innovative, locally inspired designs that capture the essence of Killarney, the town's diverse souvenir offerings promise to provide a lasting reminder of your visit to this enchanting corner of the Emerald Isle.

LOCAL CRAFTS

As you wander the quaint streets of Killarney, you'll be captivated by the variety of local craft shops and studios showcasing the remarkable talents of the region's artisans. These centers of artistic expression provide a unique glimpse into the artistic traditions and time-honored techniques that have been passed down through generations, with each piece serving as a testament to the Emerald Isle's unique cultural heritage.

Irish knitwear: One of Killarney's most iconic local crafts is renowned Irish knitwear, a centuries-old tradition that continues to captivate visitors from all over the world. Killarney's skilled knitters have mastered the art of creating luxurious, high-quality garments, ranging from the iconic

Aran sweater to intricate lace shawls and cozy woolen socks. Visitors can immerse themselves in this rich tradition by visiting the region's numerous knitwear workshops and boutiques, where they can watch local artisans meticulously work and even commission custom-made pieces to take home as treasured souvenirs.

Crystal and glassware: Killarney is also known for its exceptional crystal and glassware, which has a long history of skilled artisanship and has earned the region a reputation for producing some of the best examples of this craft in the world. Visitors can admire the delicate, intricate designs and mesmerizing interplay of light and shadow as they explore Killarney's renowned crystal and glassware makers' workshops and showrooms. From the iconic Waterford Crystal, with its timeless elegance and exquisite patterns, to the innovative and avant-garde creations of local studios, Killarney's crystal and glassware are true masterpieces, with each piece reflecting the region's artistic heritage.

Pottery and Ceramics: Killarney's rolling hills, rugged coastlines, and lush, verdant landscapes have long inspired the region's talented potters and ceramicists to create stunning, functional works of art that reflect the natural beauty of their surroundings. Visitors can wander through the charming studios and galleries of Killarney's ceramic artisans, witnessing the meticulous process of shaping, glazing, and firing the clay, and even try their hand at the potter's wheel. Killarney's pottery and ceramics range from whimsical, nature-inspired designs to elegant, minimalist pieces, reflecting the region's artistic spirit and the deep connection between local craftspeople and the land they call home.

Weaving and textiles: Killarney's rich textile heritage is another pillar of the region's artisanal landscape, with skilled weavers and textile artists producing a wide range of products, from vibrant woolen blankets and rugs to intricate, handwoven tapestries. Visitors can immerse themselves in the textile production process by visiting the region's weaving workshops and studios, where they can observe the intricate machinery and techniques used to create these beautiful, functional works of art. Many of these artisans also provide workshops and classes where visitors can try their hand at traditional weaving, embroidery, and other textile-based crafts.

Killarney's local crafts are more than just artistic expressions; they are a living, breathing testament to the region's cultural identity and the resilience of its artisanal community. These skilled craftspeople are not only creating beautiful, functional objects, but they are also preserving their ancestors' legacy by passing down time-honored techniques and traditions to future generations. Visitors who support Killarney's local craft scene not only take home a piece of the Emerald Isle's unique heritage but also help to ensure that these cultural treasures are preserved for future generations. Whether it's a cozy Aran sweater, a delicate crystal vase, or a vibrant, handwoven tapestry, Killarney crafts provide a tangible link to Ireland's rich artistic past and present.

As you wander the charming streets and vibrant craft studios of Killarney, you will be captivated by the region's deep-rooted artistic traditions and the exceptional talents of its skilled artisans. From intricate knitwear to mesmerizing crystal and glassware, Killarney's local crafts provide a truly immersive and enriching cultural experience, allowing visitors to connect with the heart and soul of this remarkable corner of Ireland.

MARKETS

The Killarney Market, held every Friday in the heart of town, is a must-see for visitors looking for an authentic taste of Irish culture and food. This vibrant marketplace, which sprawls across the historic Glebe car park, features a diverse range of local producers, artisans, and small businesses, each offering a one-of-a-kind and tempting selection of goods.

As you walk through the bustling stalls, you'll be greeted by the tantalizing aromas of freshly baked bread, the vibrant colors of locally grown produce, and the friendly faces of the enthusiastic vendors who take great pride in their offerings. From succulent meats and artisanal cheeses to handcrafted jewelry, pottery, and textiles, the Killarney Market is a veritable treasure trove of local delights, allowing visitors to interact directly with the talented makers and growers who call this region home.

Aside from the culinary and craft delights, the Killarney Market is also a hub of community and cultural exchange, with live music, street food vendors, and lively conversations that encapsulate the town's warm and welcoming spirit.

Throughout the year, Killarney hosts a variety of specialty markets and fairs, each of which provides visitors with a unique and immersive experience. The Killarney Craft Fair, held several times a year, highlights the exceptional talents of local artisans and makers, including skilled potters and weavers, jewelry designers, and wood carvers. Visitors can browse the stunning handcrafted items, interact with the creators, and even watch live demonstrations, providing a truly intimate and enriching experience with the region's thriving creative community.

The Killarney Farmers' Market, held on Saturdays in the town center, celebrates the local agricultural bounty. There is an abundance of fresh, seasonal produce here, from crisp vegetables and juicy fruits to specialty baked goods and preserves, all carefully cultivated by the hardworking farmers and producers who live in Killarney and the surrounding Kerry countryside. These specialized markets not only provide an opportunity to support local businesses and sample the best local fare, but they also serve as a community engagement hub, allowing visitors to immerse themselves in Killarney's vibrant social and cultural fabric. Visiting Killarney's markets is a truly immersive and rewarding experience, but there are a few important tips and considerations to keep in mind to ensure a smooth and enjoyable trip. The Killarney Market and other specialty markets follow set schedules, so plan your visit accordingly. Check the local event calendars and schedule your trip around market days to make the most of your time in Killarney. Many of Killarney's markets are in the town center, which can be busy and congested. Consider arriving early or taking public transportation to avoid parking issues and have a stress-free experience.

The vendors at the Killarney markets are enthusiastic about their crafts and products, and they relish the opportunity to share their stories and knowledge with customers. Do not be afraid to interact with the sellers, ask questions, and soak up the vibrant atmosphere. While some vendors accept credit cards, it is recommended that you bring cash because many of the smaller stalls and artisanal producers prefer cash transactions. This also allows you to take advantage of any special cash-only promotions or discounts. Killarney's markets are more than just a collection of stalls and vendors; they are a tapestry of local flavor, tradition, and community that captures the essence of this charming Irish town.

CHAPTER 8

PRACTICAL INFORMATION

STAYING CONNECTED: INTERNET AND MOBILE COMMUNICATION.

Killarney has made significant progress in providing reliable and widespread internet access for both residents and visitors. The town has a strong telecommunications infrastructure, with several options for accessing the internet during your stay. Killarney has numerous free public Wi-Fi hotspots located in key areas of the town. These hotspots are available in popular tourist destinations, cafes, pubs, and hotels, allowing you to stay connected while on the go.

Killarney's accommodations, including hotels, B&Bs, and self-catering apartments, offer complimentary wireless internet access to guests. This allows you to stay connected and share your experiences with friends and family back home. Ireland has a robust mobile network infrastructure, including in Killarney. The major telecommunications providers, such as Vodafone, Three, and Eir, provide extensive coverage throughout the town and surrounding area, allowing you to access the internet and stay connected using your smartphone or mobile device. In today's digital age, the ability to work or study remotely is becoming more important.

Killarney, with its stunning natural landscapes and vibrant community, has emerged as a desirable destination for those looking to balance work and leisure. The town offers several well-equipped co-working spaces for digital nomads, remote workers, and students. These shared office environments offer high-speed internet, private meeting rooms, and a professional atmosphere to ensure productivity during your stay.

Killarney provides remote learning resources and facilities for those visiting for education or training. Many local educational institutions, including Munster Technological University, offer computer labs, high-speed internet, and collaborative study spaces to visiting students. To ensure a seamless and enjoyable digital experience during your time in Killarney, here are some useful tips and considerations:

I. Research your accommodation's internet capabilities: When booking your stay, ask about the Wi-Fi quality and speed to ensure it meets your requirements.

II. Bring a portable charger or power bank: With the increased reliance on digital devices, a portable power source can be a lifesaver, especially during long outdoor excursions.

III. Consider a local SIM card or international roaming plan: If you intend to rely heavily on mobile data, purchasing a local SIM card or activating an international roaming plan can provide you with dependable and cost-effective connectivity.

IV. Familiarize yourself with backup options: If you experience unexpected connectivity issues, be aware of alternative options for accessing the internet, such as internet cafes or libraries.

V. Respect local etiquette: When using public Wi-Fi or sharing communal spaces, be considerate of others and adhere to any applicable guidelines or rules.

Killarney's commitment to providing excellent digital connectivity enables visitors to seamlessly incorporate technology into their travel experience. Whether you're a remote worker, a student, or just a curious explorer, you can be confident that staying connected in Killarney is not only possible but also a seamless and enjoyable part of your trip through this enchanting corner of Ireland. So, as you plan your trip to Killarney, take comfort in knowing that you can easily navigate the digital landscape, capturing, sharing, and cherishing your memories of this captivating destination.

LAWS AND REGULATIONS

Killarney and the rest of County Kerry are under the jurisdiction of the Republic of Ireland, so visitors are subject to the same laws and regulations that apply throughout the country. This includes adhering to national laws and regulations governing public safety, environmental protection, and cultural heritage preservation.

Furthermore, Killarney and the Killarney National Park have specific local bylaws and regulations in place to address the unique challenges and considerations of this popular tourist attraction.

These rules and guidelines are intended to ensure the sustainable management of the area's natural resources, protect the well-being of both visitors and residents and preserve the unique character and charm that make Killarney such a popular destination.

I. Environmental Protection: Killarney National Park and surrounding areas are protected natural environments, so visitors must tread lightly and respect fragile ecosystems. This includes following designated paths, avoiding littering, and not disrupting or harming the local flora and fauna. Fishing and hunting are strictly regulated, with permits and licenses required for specific activities. Before engaging in these activities, visitors should become familiar with the applicable regulations.

II. Cultural Heritage Preservation: Killarney has numerous historic sites, monuments, and heritage buildings that are legally protected. Visitors are not allowed to damage or deface cultural assets and should avoid unauthorized access or entry. Visitors are also expected to respect local traditions, customs, and ways of life, as well as refrain from engaging in disruptive or disrespectful behavior.

III. Public Safety and Order: Killarney's vibrant atmosphere, especially in the evenings, requires visitors to behave respectfully and responsibly. Excessive noise, public intoxication, and disorderly behavior are prohibited and may have legal consequences.

Visitors should also be aware of traffic laws and regulations, as well as the rules governing public transportation and parking in town and at the national park.

IV. Permitting and Licensing: Some activities and experiences in Killarney and Killarney National Park may require special permits or licenses, such as guided tours, boat rentals, and use of specific facilities or trails. - Visitors should conduct research and obtain the necessary permits or licenses before participating in these activities to avoid any legal issues or disruptions to their visit.

Adherence to Killarney's laws and regulations is more than just legal compliance; it is also a way to show respect for the local community, the natural environment, and the region's rich cultural heritage. Visitors can ensure that their time in Killarney is both enjoyable and responsible by becoming acquainted with the applicable rules and guidelines, thereby contributing to the long-term development and preservation of this exceptional destination. Visitors who fail to follow the laws and regulations may face a variety of penalties, including fines, legal proceedings, and even denial of access to certain areas or activities.

As a result, all visitors to Killarney must thoroughly educate themselves and behave responsibly, respectfully, and informally. By embracing the spirit of Killarney's laws and regulations, visitors can help to maintain the delicate balance between tourism and conservation, ensuring that this captivating corner of Ireland continues to be a source of wonder and inspiration for future generations.

CURRENCY AND MONEY-SAVING TIPS

When planning a trip to Ireland's enchanting town of Killarney, travelers must first understand the local currency and then explore effective strategies for saving money during their stay. This comprehensive guide will provide you with all of the information you need to plan a financially responsible and enjoyable Killarney adventure.

Killarney, like the rest of Ireland, has the euro as its official currency. This means that the Euro (€) is the accepted currency for all goods and services in the town and surrounding area. Travelers should be aware of the current exchange rate between their home currency and the Euro, as this can have a significant impact on purchasing power and budgeting. One of the most convenient ways to get Euros in Killarney is to use the town's numerous ATMs. These machines typically provide competitive exchange rates and allow you to withdraw cash when needed. Killarney has several currency exchange bureaus, which are often located near tourist attractions and transportation hubs.

These can be useful for exchanging large sums of money, but be aware of any fees or commission charges. Most Killarney businesses accept major credit and debit cards, including Visa, MasterCard, and American Express. This can be a convenient way to make purchases but keep in mind that your card provider may charge foreign transaction fees.

Killarney is a popular tourist destination, but with some careful planning and budgeting, you can make the most of your trip while keeping costs low. Here are some effective ways to save money during your stay in Killarney:

I. Accommodation: Look into a variety of options, including low-cost hostels and bed and breakfasts, as well as more affordable vacation rentals. Booking in advance can also help you get better rates.

II. Transportation: Take advantage of Killarney's compact size by exploring the town on foot whenever possible. If necessary, take the local bus system or consider renting bicycles, which can be a cost-effective and environmentally friendly way to get around.

III. Dining: Look for local pubs and cafes that serve traditional Irish cuisine at reasonable prices. Avoid heavily touristed areas, as menu prices tend to be higher. Consider self-catering by visiting local markets or grocery stores and preparing some of your meals.

IV. Activities and Attractions: Look into free or low-cost activities like hiking in Killarney National Park, visiting historic sites, or exploring the town's picturesque streets and squares. Many of Killarney's top attractions provide discounted tickets for students, seniors, and families.

V. Seasonal Considerations: Visiting Killarney in the shoulder or off-season (spring and fall) can result in lower lodging and transportation costs, as well as fewer visitors.

VI. Loyalty Programs: If you belong to any travel loyalty programs, such as airline or hotel rewards, make sure to use them during your stay in Killarney to earn points or miles that can be redeemed for future travel.

VII. Budgeting and Currency Conversion: Keep track of your expenses and monitor the exchange rate to ensure you're getting the most out of your travel budget. Consider using a budgeting app or carrying a travel-friendly debit/credit card with low exchange rates and fees.

Understanding the local currency and implementing savvy budgeting techniques will allow you to fully immerse yourself in the enchanting town of Killarney while also ensuring that your travel experience is both financially responsible and extremely rewarding.

SAFETY AND SECURITY

Killarney, a premier tourist destination in the heart of Ireland, is well-known for its stunning natural beauty, rich cultural heritage, and abundance of attractions, as well as its exceptional safety and security measures. Visitors to this enchanting town can be confident that their safety and the security of their belongings are of the utmost importance to both the local authorities and the community as a whole.

Killarney's commitment to the safety and security of its residents and visitors is deeply ingrained in the town's culture. This dedication is evident in the various measures and initiatives put in place to ensure a safe and secure environment for all who visit this captivating corner of Ireland. The Killarney Garda Station (Irish police force) has a strong presence in the town and patrols the streets to ensure community safety. The station is well-equipped to respond to any emergencies or incidents that may arise, and its personnel have received extensive training in providing aid and assistance to those in need.

In addition to the Garda, Killarney has a well-staffed fire department and a reliable emergency medical service, ensuring that visitors receive prompt and professional assistance in the event of an emergency. Killarney has invested heavily in public safety measures, such as well-lit streets, CCTV surveillance systems, and strategically placed emergency call boxes. These initiatives, combined with the Garda's strong presence, help visitors feel more secure and reassured. Furthermore, the town's infrastructure is well-kept, with local officials prioritizing the upkeep of roads, pavements, and other public spaces to reduce the risk of accidents or injuries. Killarney is known for its low crime rates and focus on crime prevention, making it one of Ireland's safest towns. The local authorities collaborate closely with the community to raise awareness and encourage vigilance, providing residents and visitors with information on best practices for personal safety and property protection. Visitors are advised to use the same caution and common sense as they would in any other destination, such as keeping valuables safe, avoiding isolated areas at night, and reporting any suspicious activity to the appropriate authorities.

Killarney offers exceptional support and assistance to visitors, making their stay safe, enjoyable, and memorable. The town has a network of well-trained tourism professionals, including guides, information centers, and hospitality staff, who are dedicated to assisting visitors with navigating the area, accessing local resources, and resolving any concerns or issues that may arise during their stay. Furthermore, Killarney has strong partnerships with international travel organizations and emergency assistance providers, ensuring that visitors have access to a comprehensive support network if they need it.

Killarney's unwavering commitment to safety and security, combined with its breathtaking natural beauty, rich cultural heritage, and friendly locals, make it an ideal destination for travelers looking for a truly wonderful and worry-free experience in the heart of Ireland.

HEALTH AND MEDICAL ASSISTANCE

I. General Practitioners (GPs) and Clinics: Killarney offers a variety of primary care services, including routine check-ups, prescription refills, and minor illness/injury treatment. These clinics are typically open during regular business hours and easily accessible to visitors.

II. Pharmacies: Killarney has numerous local pharmacies that offer prescriptions, over-the-counter medications, first-aid supplies, and healthcare products. Many pharmacies in town provide basic health services like blood pressure checks and flu vaccinations.

III. Hospitals and Emergency Care: Killarney offers a modern, well-equipped hospital, University Hospital Kerry, for medical emergencies or specialized care. This facility offers a wide range of medical services, including an emergency department, inpatient care, and specialized clinics. Furthermore, the town has several ambulance services that can respond quickly to emergencies.

As a visitor to Killarney, you will have several options for receiving medical care and assistance during your stay. To ensure a smooth and stress-free trip, become familiar with these options ahead of time.

I. Travel Insurance: Ensure you have comprehensive travel insurance that covers medical expenses, emergency care, and repatriation. This will give you peace of mind and help you avoid unexpected medical expenses during your trip.

II. European Health Insurance Card (EHIC): Citizens of the European Union may be eligible for the EHIC, which allows them to access state-provided healthcare in Ireland at the same cost as Irish residents. Make sure you get your EHIC before your trip and keep it with you at all times.

III. Private Healthcare Providers: Killarney offers a variety of private healthcare options, including hospitals, clinics, and specialists. While these services may be more expensive, they offer more personalized attention and shorter wait times.

IV. Language Assistance: Killarney's healthcare professionals are highly skilled and trained to assist international visitors. If you are concerned about language barriers, many healthcare facilities in town can provide translation services or arrange for interpreters to ensure effective communication.

To ensure a smooth and worry-free healthcare experience during your visit to Killarney, take the following proactive steps:

- Before your trip, research and locate the nearest healthcare facilities, clinics, and pharmacies.
- Make sure you have adequate travel insurance and, if applicable, carry your EHIC. Pack any necessary medications, as well as a record of your medical history and current conditions.
- Familiarize yourself with Killarney's emergency numbers and procedures.
- Consider downloading any healthcare apps or digital tools that will help you during your stay.

Killarney's commitment to providing high-quality healthcare and medical assistance allows visitors to enjoy the town's many attractions and experiences without worry. You can be confident that your health and well-being will be in good hands during your visit to this enchanting corner of Ireland if you take the initiative and become acquainted with the available resources.

SUSTAINABLE TOURISM

Killarney's commitment to sustainable tourism is multifaceted, encompassing a wide range of initiatives and partnerships, all aimed at ensuring the long-term viability and vitality of the region's natural and cultural resources. Killarney has implemented a comprehensive environmental management plan aimed at reducing waste, conserving water and energy, and promoting biodiversity. This includes recycling programs, the use of renewable energy sources, and the preservation of sensitive habitats and ecosystems.

Killarney has made a concerted effort to preserve and celebrate the region's rich cultural heritage, including traditions, crafts, and historical sites. This includes supporting local artisans, preserving historic landmarks, and offering educational opportunities for visitors to learn about the region's rich history.

Killarney's sustainable tourism initiative is a collaborative effort that includes the local community, businesses, and government organizations. Killarney has been able to develop tourism strategies that balance visitor needs with resident concerns and priorities by encouraging partnerships and open communication. Killarney has made investments in sustainable modes of transportation, such as electric shuttle buses, bike-sharing programs, and well-developed pedestrian and cycling infrastructure. This not only reduces visitors' carbon footprints, but also improves the overall experience by encouraging exploration on a smaller, more personal scale.

Killarney's tourism industry has adopted a variety of responsible practices, including the use of eco-friendly accommodations and tour operators, as well as the promotion of low-impact activities and the encouragement of visitors to follow "leave no trace" guidelines. Killarney's dedication to sustainable tourism is most visible in its approach to promoting the region's natural wonders.

From the captivating Killarney Lakes and the dramatic Skellig Islands to the rugged beauty of the Ring of Kerry, Killarney has devised novel ways for visitors to enjoy these iconic landscapes while minimizing their environmental impact.

I. Guided Tours and Educational Experiences: Killarney tour operators have adopted sustainable practices, providing guided tours that teach visitors about the region's fragile ecosystems, local conservation efforts, and the value of responsible tourism.

II. Trails and Pathways: Killarney has invested in a vast network of well-kept trails and pathways, encouraging visitors to explore the region on foot or by bicycle, resulting in a more intimate and sustainable connection with the natural environment.

III. Visitor Management: In sensitive areas, such as the Skellig Islands, Killarney has implemented visitor management systems that limit the number of people allowed to enter at any given time, ensuring the preservation of these unique and fragile environments.

IV. Sustainable Accommodations: Killarney's hospitality industry has embraced eco-friendly practices, with an increasing number of properties obtaining sustainability certifications and implementing initiatives to reduce their environmental impact.

Killarney's commitment to sustainable tourism is an ongoing process that necessitates continuous innovation, collaboration, and the unwavering dedication of the entire community. As the region evolves and adapts to the changing needs of visitors, it remains committed to preserving the natural and cultural treasures that have made it a popular destination for generations.

Killarney sets a shining example for other destinations around the world by embracing the principles of sustainable tourism, demonstrating that it is possible to balance visitor needs with the imperative to protect the Emerald Isle's fragile and irreplaceable natural resources. Killarney's holistic approach ensures that its natural wonders, rich cultural heritage, and warm hospitality will continue to captivate and inspire visitors for many years to come.

USEFUL PHRASES IN IRISH GAELIC

While English is widely spoken in Killarney and the rest of Ireland, Irish Gaelic remains an important part of the local culture. From street signs and menus to casual conversations, the melodic cadence of the Gaelic language can be heard echoing through the streets, inviting visitors to immerse themselves in this captivating culture.

By learning a few key Irish Gaelic phrases, you'll not only be able to navigate Killarney more easily, but you'll also be able to form meaningful connections with the locals, who will undoubtedly appreciate your efforts to engage with their language. While immersing yourself in the enchanting world of Killarney, consider incorporating these useful Irish Gaelic phrases into your daily interactions:

Greetings and Introductions:
- Hello: Dia dhuit (DEE-ah witch).
- Good morning: Maidin mhaith (MAH-jin wah).
- Good afternoon: Tráthnóna maith (TRAH-no-nah mah).
- Good evening: Oíche mhaith (EE-heh wah).
- My name is...: Is mise ... (ISS mish-eh...).

- Pleased to meet you: Tá áthas orm do bheith ag.../Tá sé go hiontach bualadh libh (TAH AH-hass orm duh veh ag... / TAH shay guh HIN-tuck BOOL-uh liv)

Basic Conversational Phrases:
- How are you? Cén chaoi a bhfuil tú? (KEN hee ah VIL too?).
- I'm well, thank you: Tá mé go maith, go raibh maith agat (TAH may guh MAH, guh rah mah ah-gut).
- Do you speak English? An bhfuil Béarla agat? (un will BEAR-lah ah-gut?).
- I don't understand: Ní thuigim (NEE hig-im).
- Please: Le do thoil (leh duh hil).
- Thank you: Go raibh maith agat (guh rah mah ah-gut).
- You're welcome: Tá fáilte romhat (TAH FAL-cheh ROH-wut).

Ordering and Dining:
- I would like...: Ba mhaith liom... (bah wah lum...).
- A pint of Guinness, please: Pionta Guinness, le do thoil (PEEN-tah Gin-iss, leh duh hil).

- The bill, please: An bhille le do thoil (un BIL-eh leh duh hil).

Exploring and Sightseeing:
- Where is...: Cá bhfuil...? (kah will...).
- Directions: Treoracha (TRER-ah-kuh).
- Beautiful: Álainn (AHL-in).
- Wonderful: Iontach (IN-tuhk).

Learning and incorporating these essential Irish Gaelic phrases into your travels in Killarney will not only improve your ability to navigate the local landscape but will also lead to a deeper, more meaningful connection with the people and culture of this incredible region.

The act of speaking the native tongue, even if only for a few words, will be warmly welcomed by the locals, who will appreciate your efforts to immerse yourself in their culture. This simple gesture has the potential to spark genuine connections, unforgettable experiences, and a greater appreciation for Killarney's rich tapestry of Irish culture.

CONCLUSION

As you near the end of this comprehensive travel guide to the enchanting region of Killarney, Ireland, we want to express our heartfelt gratitude for joining us on this captivating journey. Through the pages of this guide, we have attempted to reveal the captivating tapestry of natural beauty, rich cultural heritage, and limitless adventure opportunities that make Killarney and its surrounding areas a true jewel in the crown of the Emerald Isle. We hope that the awe-inspiring grandeur of the Gap of Dunloe, the mystical allure of the Skellig Islands, and the serene splendor of the Killarney Lakes have inspired you to go out and explore the myriad wonders that this remarkable region has to offer.

Our goal in sharing our expertise and insights has been to provide you with the knowledge and practical information you need to make the most of your time in Killarney, ensuring that your journey is not only full of breathtaking sights but also imbued with a deeper understanding and appreciation for the rich tapestry of Irish culture and tradition.

As you plan your trip and set your sights on Killarney's breathtaking landscapes, we invite you to embrace the spirit of adventure, the call of the wild, and the timeless charm that has captivated visitors for generations. May your journey be one of discovery, wonder, and lasting memories. Thank you for choosing to discover the enchanting world of Killarney, Ireland. We eagerly await the opportunity to welcome you to this exceptional corner of the Emerald Isle, where nature's beauty and the warmth of the human spirit combine to create an experience that will live long in your heart and mind.

WOULD YOU LIKE TO GET INSTANT ACCESS TO MORE TRAVEL GUIDE BOOKS BY THE AUTHOR? SCAN THE QR CODE BELOW!

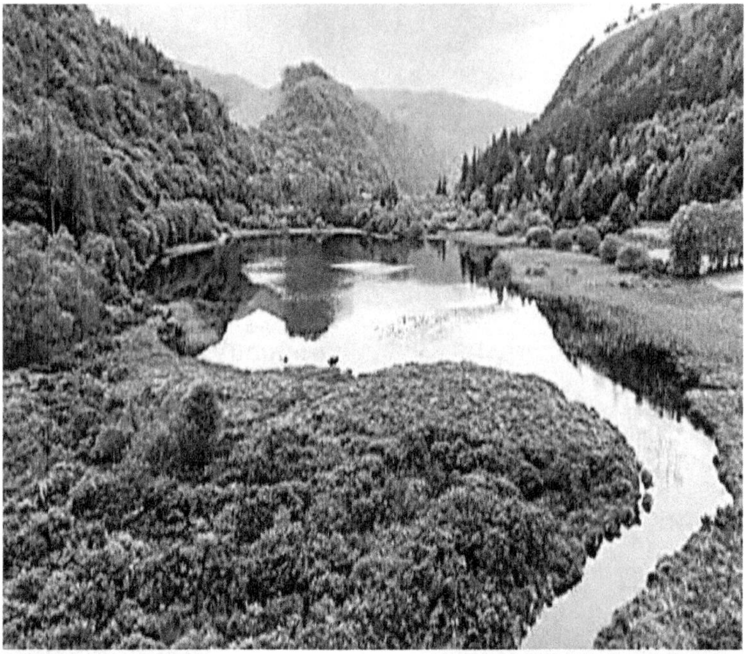

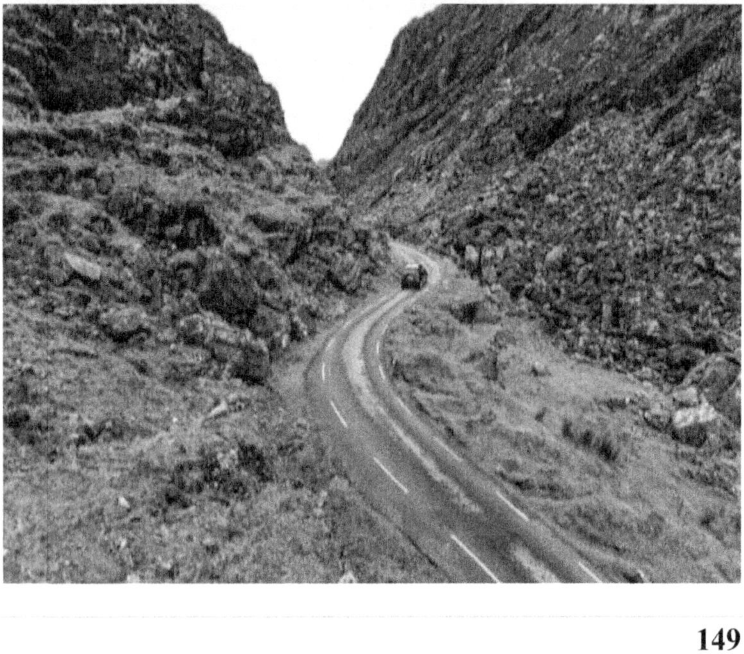

Printed in Dunstable, United Kingdom